10 HABITS FOR GRIEF AND LOSS

CREATE CHANGE THROUGH ADVERSITY TO
BECOME A BETTER YOU

CORTEZ RANIERI

CONTENTS

DEDICATION

For my late mother, Maureen Ranieri. Not a day goes by where I don't think about you. I'll cherish the time we spent together for the rest of my life. I love and miss you always. I'll see you on the other side angel.

INTRODUCTION

It was November 24th, 2007. I was abruptly woken up by my aunt. Her eyes were filled with tears as she struggled to get the words out, "Cortez, she's gone. Your mom has finally let go, and she's passed away." I rubbed my eyes, continuously opening and closing them, hoping I was in a bad dream. It turns out, I wasn't. Reality had set in and my mom's two-year battle with cancer had finally ended. This was a day I knew was coming but could never fully prepare for.

As I walked upstairs into her room, my family surrounded my mom's lifeless body. They all looked back at me with tears in their eyes. My knees became weak and my chest tightened up. As I got closer, I saw my mom lying on a hospital bed with her eyes closed. I kneeled beside her, grabbed her hand, praying she would hold mine back, but there was nothing. This reassured me she was gone. My eyes filled with tears as I laid my head on her chest and said my last goodbye. I was 14-years old at the time and I thought I was prepared for this, but fate proved me wrong. However, I saw I was not the only one in grief. Despite feeling lost and struggling to breathe through my overwhelmed chest, I resolved to do everything I could to heal and, perhaps, help those around me heal too. Since then, I've lost all my grandparents as well as two friends and have learned many things about death that I want to share with others.

Grief has a remarkable tendency to make us feel alone, yet we're never truly alone in knowing the experience of grief. Death is one of the most frequent causes of long-term grief, but it is not the only one. Maybe the love of your life abandoned you. Maybe your parents split up, and now live a world apart from each other. Or maybe you've recently begun living thousands of miles away from a childhood friend you used to visit every day.

It does not matter if the cause of your grief is big or small compared to those around you, you're still allowed to feel the associated guilt if you think you could've done something better. You're still allowed to acknowledge the sense of helplessness if the cause of grief was never something you chose. You're still allowed to experience regret if you did choose, only to wish you could still go back. Most of all, you're allowed to feel alone, even if you spend each and every day in a room full of people. Loneliness isn't determined by how many or how few people are in a room with us. It's determined by who we wish was still there.

However, all these feelings are only one side of a coin. You wouldn't be reading this book if you weren't willing to try and get back to how you used to be before your tragedy happened. You won't ever be like you were before; instead, you'll be better. Helping you achieve mental clarity and helping you nurture your inner strength is my primary concern throughout this book. I resolve to help you regain control over your life. Imagine a life where you are strong despite your wounds. Imagine a life where, even though you may feel helpless from time to time, you're able to recover and make the best of what's left going forward. Imagine a life where your pain ceases to be nothing but a reminder of what you lost; imagine a life where your pain can become a way for you to reach out and comfort those you love. But first, imagine a life where you are able to reach out and comfort yourself.

To these ends, I will show you ten strategies, each of which are geared towards strengthening your soul. You will learn exactly how to take the pain and adversity in your life and transform it from a debilitating problem into an opportunity for growth.

If anyone has ever frustrated you with the words "misery builds character," only to then leave you miserable on your own, I will show you how to persevere until those words transform into something more helpful. Suffering alone does not promote growth, but what you'll learn shall ensure that your pains will not be for naught.

But why does showing you all of this matter so much to me? Why is it so important that I share all I know about dealing with grief? As I said, I felt lost and overwhelmed after losing my mother. I tried a lot of things; I tried talking to people, I tried not talking to people. For a while, I barely ate at all. I indulged in stacks of comfort food, like heavy, high-GI (glycemic index) carbs and sweets. I've tried music, and I've tried silence. In the beginning, I was just a kid. It took me many years to come up with a system that worked in soothing my grief.

After testing many, many more habits as I was growing up, the ones I've finally included in this book are those that I continue practicing, even as a fully-matured adult. Even after coming to terms with my grief, what's written in the chapters of this book continue to help me in my day to day life. Because of this, I strongly believe that these ten tips will help you, too.

The reason I share them with you now is that I know not everyone has been able to take the time to figure things out in the years since age fourteen. Let my trials help you heal, and hopefully cut a clearer path through a confusion similar to the one I once had to walk through.

Now more than ever, it is important that you make time for yourself, be gentle with yourself, and most of all, show care to yourself. For some people, grief is an illness that must be eradicated. For other people, it's simply part of the human condition that needs to be understood. Regardless of how you view grief, it's important that you take some time to maintain yourself. Join me now, and we'll start somewhere simple; maintaining your body.

1

MOVE YOUR BODY

One of the easiest ways to maintain your body is through exercise. To some people, exercise means working yourself to death, performing several laps around the block, or climbing to the top of a tall rope. This is not what we're aiming for. We are exercising not only to get more fit but to clear our heads.

Now, exercise will not snuff out your grief, but it is still essential for helping you cope with loss. Physical exercise is one of the best ways to release endogenous endorphins into your bloodstream. When released, these endorphins help your body cope with pain as well as help your mind find calmness. Unlike alternative methods of numbing pain, such as alcohol, your endorphins are not addictive, will not impair your awareness, will not create delusions, and will never cause feelings of dependency. In reality, because your endorphins are a product of your body rather than an external crutch, using their natural release to boost yourself is one of the most empowering things you can do in times of helplessness.

It is no wonder, then, that exercise is often suggested as a healthy way to combat depression. However, it's not as simple as that. For a start, grief and depression are not the same thing, even if society at large tends to use the two words interchangeably. Medically, depression is indicated by persistent sadness and a noticeable decrease in pleasure from life or activities, including hobbies you normally enjoy.

Depression can mean slower movements, indecisiveness, apathy toward death, loss of hunger, poor sleep, or an overwhelming feeling of worthlessness, paranoia or guilt. You do not need to be conscious of what's making you depressed to experience depression and, the more severe your depression is, the more of these symptoms you'll experience at the same time (Knott, 2017).

Grief, meanwhile, is explicitly an intense pain caused by the feeling of loss, especially when it's the loss of a friend or loved one.

However, grief can turn into what's medically termed as *complicated grief. Complicated grief* is defined as a powerful physical and emotional reaction to a loss that persists for a long time, potentially even years (Smith, 2018). Symptoms are largely similar to those of depression, with the added bite of experiencing intense pain whenever you think of what you lost. Complicating the matter is the fact that, during grief, it can be difficult to think of anything else. It's no surprise that experiencing such intense pain for so long can easily cause a downward spiral into depression itself.

Exercise, then, lets you deal with grief while preventing you from being swallowed up in complicated grief and, by extension, depression. However, even if you are already exhibiting symptoms of depression, do not fret. It's not too late to start getting your endorphins going and erode the malaise of despair.

Even as little as one hour of exercise per week can help alleviate the effects of complicated grief or depression (Harvey *et al*, 2017), allowing you to tackle your true grief in an uncluttered, healthy fashion.

HOW TO BEGIN: THE MINDSET

Of course, grief is deeply taxing not just on a mental level, but on a physical level too. The intense sadness we feel in response to loss can leave us feeling exhausted, on top of shutting down our normal self-care routines. When this happens, how on earth do we galvanize ourselves? Where do we find the motivation to begin exercising again? What if we never exercised even before the grief?

The trick is to start small. An hour is only 60 minutes. That can be broken up into 10-minute bouts across 6 days of the week, with a 1-day sabbath. That's half the length of a kid's cartoon show per day. You could even spend those 10 minutes of exercise in front of the TV while watching a cartoon show, if that's what you enjoy.

Grief does not affect us all in the same way, so choose something that's just a slight tad outside of your comfort zone. If your grief has caused you to shut yourself in isolation, allow your exercise to be a brief walk to your mailbox and back. When you return to your couch, your bed, or wherever you sit when you contemplate your grief, consider performing a stretch before laying down. When you engage in exercise, you help take your focus off your pain for a little while.

Now, when you're grieving, it is understandable that you might not want to take your mind off your loss and, by extension, you might not want to do anything that shifts your focus. You might even see shifting focus as bad. Consider why you might feel that way. For me, I found it difficult to shift my focus off my grief because, on a deep level, I felt that if I took my mind off who I lost, then I'd lose them completely. Of course, this isn't true; even after all these years, I can remember the way my mother's laugh made me feel, or the memories I shared with some of my late friends as we speculated on our futures and dreams. But, at the time, I was adamant that I wouldn't do anything that resembled actually letting go.

However, sometimes a shift in focus is exactly what we need. Shifting focus is what lets us take a step back and get a better view of the big picture. When we experience *complicated grief*, we trigger two things: the "reward" parts of our brain, and the "avoidance" parts of our brain (Jewell, 2014). In hindsight, this explains much of why I felt as I did at the time. I was constantly longing for the "reward" of seeing my mother again, every time I thought of her. But, of course, that reward would never truly be satisfied. I'd see pictures or videos of her, of course, but those never felt fully like *her*. If anything, they just highlighted her absence. But still, the "reward" part of my brain kept flashing, creating a yearning.

Eventually, I became addicted to the thought of her presence. Now, I wasn't ready to confront her loss yet by any means, blame the "avoidance" part of my brain firing up all the time, but working out helped me get closer to where I needed to be.

For a while, I exercised entirely on my own. The "avoidance" part of my brain kept me away from other people. I couldn't bear the thought of perhaps one day losing them too. At that age, it didn't occur to me that by cutting myself off from everyone the way I had, I'd effectively lost them all already.

The shifting focus caused by my exercise sessions slowly helped me realize how self-defeating my thinking was. Before this realization, I'd sometimes spend about a quarter of an hour walking around a field near where I lived, ruminating on how awful life was and how worthless I felt for not being a better son. What I didn't realize at the time was that the more I kept walking, the more I was telling myself that I still had some power over my body. No matter what was on my mind, I could still trust my feet.

I considered the world I was walking around in. I didn't really want to be in it. I never asked to be in a world without my mother. That wasn't my choice. But it was my choice to walk around in this field. It was my choice as to where I'd put my feet next. More and more, I began to visit this field, until I was there almost every day.

More and more, I gradually began to feel at least on a subconscious level that although I didn't like where I was, or where I'd been, I could still decide where to go from there. For a while, I began to feel a little better. And then winter came.

During winter months, when the rain was too intense for walks, I let myself go again. I thought it was just the winter making me feel worse, but it was the lack of exercise. However, as walking felt too cold, I started to run instead. I ran to the nearby library and did sets of stairs. Although it was freezing out, my body quickly warmed up from the intense exercise. When I would return home, my *monkey mind* would be completely settled. I spotted the connection between my physical activity and sense of peace.

When I eventually figured it out, I joined a local gym. I wasn't particularly knowledgeable in working out, but after enough time shifting my focus off my grief I began realizing my body ached like hell, and not from the exercise. The strain my grief had put on my body left me feeling like an old man, and I was only in high school! I hated stretching, it was too boring for me, so the best way for me to scrape all the rust off my bones, was to create a routine. I began doing a little bit of stretching every morning when I got up, and sometimes just before I had a shower too. It didn't make me feel happier, or less anxious, but it did make me feel *better* in the sense that things didn't feel so impossible, and at that stage that's all that really mattered to me: believing that life could still be possible.

Maybe you're not a fan of lifting weights or running, but even so, I'd highly recommend at least giving yoga a try. Now, it's not something I did when my grief was at its worst, mostly because I still hated stretching back then, but when I passed into adulthood and began taking a proper look at what it meant to do yoga, I began cursing myself for ignoring it in the past. To this day, I like to perform a mini-yoga session in my bedroom before getting dressed in the morning.

TOO MUCH OF A GOOD THING

Although galvanizing yourself to perform exercise can be helpful, you must be careful not to overdo it. While a little exercise will help lift your mood and regain perspective, you must remember that your body is still hurting while you are in grief. You do not want to exercise to the point that your pain becomes worse. If you had a strenuous workout routine before your loss, do not shame yourself for letting it go. Taking a step back and giving your body a little space to rest is probably the smartest thing you can do in this case (Frey, 2019).

If you're used to rigorous physical activity, then you are more than welcome to continue as long as your body isn't fighting you. For some people, staying true to their routine is even a way of finding solace and maintaining a feeling of familiarity or security in a world that may otherwise seem very precarious. However, you are not under any obligation to continue that routine.

No matter how stringent you normally are concerning your exercise, one must note that while you are grieving, you are naturally more vulnerable to illness, clumsiness, injury, tiredness, muscle pains, and back pains. Even highly well-trained individuals such as veteran infantrymen are known to suffer from these physical symptoms while they are working through grief. If you are not performing to the same standards that you used to, do not fret. This isn't a sign that you're losing yourself, or that you've washed up. Reduced performance is natural in a time like this.

When you have not yet come to terms with your grief, it's comparable in many ways to suffering from an illness. Would you try to push your body beyond its limits while you're suffering from an illness? Failing to meet your usual exercise targets during this time does not mean that you yourself are a failure; all it means is that you're still recovering, and that's okay. Just keep doing the exercises you can. You want to feel the air fill your lungs. You want to feel a warmth spread through your muscles. You want to feel your head rarify. But you do not want to feel pain.

If you're a hardcore fitness enthusiast, you may be used to the idea of treating your fitness obstacles like brick walls for you to bulldoze through. However, right now, you are not a machine. With all the water in your body, you're an ocean. Perhaps, right now, you're a sea of tears. Take a moment to consider the ocean. It can gather up with mighty winds to become a devastating and powerful hurricane. Yet how long does that hurricane last? After a few days or less it dissipates, and the land undoes its accomplishments easily. In the end, all the hurricane does is inflict injury before fading away.

Now, consider the ocean when it is calm. It moves back and forth, rising and falling, in a gentle rhythm across the world. Yet it is this gentle rhythm that carves pillars out of the earth, builds land, defines mountains and valleys. Therefore, when you choose to exercise in grief, be like the waves, and not the hurricane. This means you should exercise every day if you can, but don't do it to drench yourself in sweat. Don't do it to burn hundreds of calories of fat. Do it to carve clarity out of your chaos.

BEING LIKE THE WAVES

Whether you're a sedentary individual just getting into exercise, or an iron titan needing to cut back for a little while, you can release your endorphins using surprisingly simple, even gentle, exercises. I prefer to keep things light while I grieve, because it lets me stay fit and get the bodily chemicals I need without straining my body or hurting it further. A light exercise has even led to a better night's sleep on multiple occasions, which was a welcome blessing for me considering how tired I felt all the time while I was still processing things.

For something easy, let's start with a brisk walk. Bring some headphones and listen to some music or a podcast. Listening to music is a popular pastime, and it's not uncommon for us to turn to it when we're feeling grief. You can put on something upbeat that motivates you to walk or pick up the pace. Having an inspirational podcast can also make the walk more enjoyable, while you're retaining information and learning something new.

If walking isn't enough, then perhaps you'll enjoy some body-weight movements or a run. You don't need equipment for this, but if you want to do a short burst workout, make sure you're warmed up first. About 2 minutes of jumping-jacks will get your muscles warm and loose. Then, give yourself about a minute to catch your breath. If you're either motivated or don't feel warm yet, feel free to repeat this process another 1-2 times.

After that, find a clear spot away from any main walking areas, and start doing some burpees. You can add in other movements, such as air squats, lunges, sit-ups or pushups. You could do 10-15 reps of each and repeat this process 4 times. If you want a more intense workout, you can repeat this process or add more reps in 1 session before the energy expended stops being worth the endorphins you're getting back. Make sure to allow yourself a full minute of total rest for every 2 minutes you spend exercising.

Do not be afraid to start small, even if you're known for being a fitness champion before your loss. There is no need to rush; simply make sure you're getting your endorphins each day. Even if you're doing much less than what is suggested, don't be ashamed. Some days all you can do is a 10-minute walk, or a short stretch before bed. Anything is better than nothing; simply do your best to keep doing "anything" consistently. If you feel safe enough to reach out to friends or acquaintances, see if you can involve them in your exercise routine as well. Their presence will be a great help in keeping you motivated to carry on, although the emphasis is on the word *help*. If you have to go it alone for a while, I believe you can do it.

If you're interested in using weights or expanding your exercise repertoire, do not be afraid to go online to search for things like weightlifting, yoga, or Pilates techniques. If you're able to get out there, join in a local group fitness class with like-minded people and feed off their energy to keep you motivated.

2

EAT WELL

Earlier, I mentioned off-hand that exercise is a better way to take the edge off emotional pain compared to, say, alcohol. But does that mean you shouldn't drink at all? And if not, what are the alternatives?

Diet is just as important as exercise. Similarly to exercise, it is also one of those things that we tend to either ignore entirely or indulge in way too much when we are grieving. If you've lost interest in food as a result of complicated grief, then you've likely lost quite a bit of weight since your loss. On the other hand, maybe you decided to dive as deep as you could into your comfort foods, and have since put on a lot of weight as a result. Some people are more fortunate than others and don't get visibly heavier from all they eat. Others are not so lucky; it's okay to be a little overweight, but social stigmas around the condition can make an already difficult situation even harder from body-shaming.

However, my advice from earlier has not changed; this is not the time to judge yourself. When we are grieving, we already feel down. Why kick ourselves while we're down by adding to the negative voices around us? Weight loss or weight gain isn't a priority right now, regardless of what people around you may be saying. The priority is helping you retain a clear mind. Luckily, exercise isn't the only thing that can contribute to this; a good diet can help you puzzle your way through your thoughts, too.

ALCOHOL, CAFFEINE, AND WATER

The first thing I cannot recommend enough is to cut down on caffeine and alcohol. When we're grieving, we dehydrate ourselves very quickly through the immense volume of tears we shed, or the cold sweats we experience from deep anxiety. Although alcohol is known as a nice distraction, and caffeine is known to give us plentiful energy, both of these substances only give their gifts for a very short amount of time. In the long-term, they can disempower you by making you feel dependent on their effects to have fun or feel alive (Frey, 2019).

What's worse, both of these substances make you pass more water from your body than they give, causing you to dehydrate even faster. This is an issue because over 75% of your brain is made up of water. Think of this water as a cooling system in a computer. If you're dehydrated, then your mind begins to become slower, begins to have greater trouble processing information and, if left untreated long enough, may even begin to overheat or crash.

Caffeine and alcohol, therefore, are not good for keeping your mind clear during grief. But that doesn't mean you can't indulge in any of these substances at all!

Much like the sweets or chocolates that one might have had as a child, unhealthy foods are fine if taken in moderation. For coffee, I highly recommend no more than 8-10 ounces each day before the mid-morning. For alcohol, it is best to have no more than 5 ounces, or 2/3rds of a cup, per week. As an adult, I like to have all 5 ounces in one day on my Sabbath, and then take pleasure from exercise instead during the other 6 days of the week.

Aside from that, I recommend drinking plenty of water. 10 cups a day is recommended. The best way for me is to have a cup as soon as I wake up to help clear my head; we still dehydrate while we're asleep, so it's important to take that edge off with a nice glass of water as soon as possible. I'll then have another cup at breakfast, lunch and dinner, and a final cup just before I brush my teeth and use the toilet in preparation for bed. I'll also have a cup just after finishing my exercise for the day. That's already 6 out of the 10 cups needed. I don't make as big a fuss about counting the other 4 these days, but I do make a point of getting up and going for a drink of water immediately if I'm battling to think, or feeling very hot or dry.

If you're struggling to cut down on the coffee or alcohol, you may wish to drink more water as a way to compensate. Staying hydrated is terribly important for your brain, and without proper hydration you'll have a difficult time processing your grief. Investing in a reusable water bottle and keeping it close by can trigger you to remember to drink water throughout the day.

PROTEINS AND MINERALS

Proteins are a vital part of your diet, allowing your cells to regenerate optimally by aiding in the DNA replication process. When we're grieving, we already feel as if we're under a lot of stress. When we're short on protein, that feeling can be magnified as cells will be more likely to replicate imperfectly or respond poorly to everyday wear-and-tear, causing a vague feeling of unwellness without there being any clear cause (Lehman, 2020). During grief, it can be a good idea to make sure at least a tenth to a third of what you're eating each day consists of protein. This could mean having a little bit of protein in each meal, or it could mean having a lump sum of protein at the end of the day. The choice is yours.

Luckily, you also have a great deal of choice in terms of what form that protein can take. Fish, poultry, and red meats are all wonderful sources of protein that are easily recognizable. For vegetarians, legumes such as peanuts, lentils and beans are a great alternative source. Eggs, yogurt, milk and cheese will also all work well for maintaining sufficient protein levels. When about 20-33% of your diet consists of these foods, your cells will have a much easier time building themselves up, which will help you feel better.

They'll also help you get the most out of your exercise by reducing the negative aspects like muscle strain, leading to a great positive knock-on effect for your physical and mental wellbeing.

Aside from protein, you can further help your body withstand the physical side of grief through taking in vitamins and minerals. This doesn't mean you need medication, of course! Vitamins can be found naturally in many of the foods around us. Spinach and bananas, for instance, contain B-complex vitamins. These vitamins are great at helping you convert your body's energy stores into usable power when needed, and helping you shake off lethargy. Most of the sources of protein listed above also contain forms of vitamin B.

Meanwhile, chili peppers, broccoli, lemons, strawberries, oranges, kale, parsley and thyme are all rich in vitamin C, a vital mineral for bolstering your immune system. Remember, your immune system has a harder time doing its job due to the way your mental stress affects your body while you grieve. Now, you cannot control when you start or stop grieving per se, but you can control what you eat during that time. It can be difficult to properly resolve grief when we keep falling ill, so in this instance, vitamin C can be a great help in letting you endure reaching into the bottom of your heart.

Vitamin D is great for reducing the aching feeling in your bones and can be gained from egg yolks, cheese, milk and salmon. Your body is also able to produce vitamin D on its own when you're out in the sun, which may be another reason why winter might cause your grief to become magnified. Being stuck indoors wasn't great for me during my grief.

Aside from vitamins and proteins, another good thing to look out for are antioxidants, which can be found in most fruits that have bright or deep colors. Antioxidants help your body in a variety of ways, such as reducing the physical stress on your heart, promoting healthy sugar conversion, and fortifying your mental health. They're also great at snatching up loose particles in your body, such as the carcinogenic compounds from smoke or the cell-damaging particles of toxins. If you've been overeating or smoking a lot during your grief, switching up your diet to include more antioxidants can help you regain control over your health.

Aside from fruit such as blueberries, strawberries, cherries, plums and apples, you can also find antioxidants in a variety of beans such as red beans, black beans, kidney beans and pinto beans. Unlike antioxidant-based medication, antioxidant-rich food has a variety of positive side-effects due to the additional nutrients they carry, on top of also being super delicious. Compare and contrast to the side-effects of some medications, which can include heightened depression, lethargy, or muddied thinking. During grief, those are the last feelings we'd want to reinforce, so as much as possible try to get your vitamins through your food instead of your pharmaceutical supplements. If you feel unsure, do not hesitate to consult a doctor to set your mind at ease. In the case of prescriptions, which are not the same as basic supplements and need to be followed to the letter to achieve safe and effective results, do not change or alter the instructions without the aid and approval of your doctor.

PREPARING FOOD AND LOOKING AFTER YOUR DIET

Even when we know what's best for ourselves, it isn't always easy to act on that information. Depending on the stage and circumstance of grief, it may be difficult to stay motivated with a diet, especially if it is different from the food we enjoyed as a kid. Macaroni and cheese, pizza, potato chips and ice cream are all infamous comfort foods. These foods are fine in moderation, but during grief we tend to overdo it a bit. Much like coffee or alcohol, excessive high-carb diets can end up just making us feel worse in the long run, especially high-GI carbs like processed cereals, white bread, corn starch or white rice.

High-GI carbohydrates and high-sucrose treats, which together make up almost all of our common "comfort" foods, tend to feel heavy in our belly, which is partially where that feeling of comfort comes from. Our bodies like to feel full, and the full-ness of a good carb can be intensely satisfying, but our stomachs can't always tell the difference between good fullness and bad fullness.

If we fill up entirely on comfort food, our blood sugar levels begin to spike and crash dramatically. Why does this matter? When our blood sugar crashes, we become lethargic and begin to feel listless, or even begin to show symptoms of depression. Our body does not react well when our blood sugar behaves like a roller-coaster, and anything that affects our body will inevitably have a knock-on effect on our minds.

High-GI carbs also have the nasty side-effect of increasing our cortisol production. While cortisol can be good for the body in small amounts, in large doses it can massively increase your risk of complicated grief or depression. The best ways to get rid of excess cortisol are through exercise and socialization. If your stage of grief doesn't permit you to perform consistent exercise or communication, however, then you will need to be extra careful with what you put in your body for the sake of your stress and anxiety levels.

Nevertheless, carbs are delicious, and you might still want to keep them as part of your diet regardless. Brown rice, rye bread, pitas, tortillas and whole-grain loaves are all great alternatives to high-GI carbs, giving that starchy feeling of comfort while having less intense sugar crashes. Combine them with the suggested sources of proteins and minerals for true healthy comfort.

As a general rule, it is best to prepare all your meals in advance. Our grief isn't always at the same level of intensity, but it often feels as if it ebbs and flows without our consent. If your grief is peaking close to mealtime, it could lead to an eating disorder. This could mean desperately getting hold of food based on nostalgia and convenience rather than nutrients. Or perhaps it could mean not feeling hungry at all even when you know you *should* be eating.

By preparing healthy meals in advance, you give yourself the freedom to make food when you're in the best mental space possible to do so. This could mean making tomorrow's breakfast and lunch at the same time you make dinner. It could mean making something during lunchtime, but only eating it later when you actually feel hungry. Or it could mean pre-cooking vast batches of rice, beans and vegetables so that whenever you're hungry you can take spoonful's of each ingredient out and just plop it on your plate, perhaps with a little seasoning.

It can mean picking a day where you feel relatively okay and simply make all your meals for the week in bulk until you're done. It can even mean putting on some soothing music and only making your food while it's playing. If it works, it works. It can take 6-12 months after a great loss to get back into a consistently healthy eating schedule, so do not give up if you're still struggling to get things done through your grief. Simply take the steps you can, and trust that the more you get into healthier habits again, the easier it'll be to stay there.

When you have a moment, make meals for yourself for the future. That way, when your grief spikes up again, you won't be forced to turn to convenience foods or takeout's. By taking care of your future self in this way, you'll have an easier time maintaining a healthy food intake, because those healthy meals will already be ready-made for you. From there, you can comfort yourself through food without having to suffer from a blood-sugar crash.

Another way to look after your diet is by keeping your changes small. Some of us may be able to switch diets to something healthier instantly, but many of us just go with what we already know. This is because, in the first stages of grief, we're sometimes required to make a lot of very difficult choices in a very small space of time. This can lead to us feeling worn out decision-wise, and contribute to that feeling of mental fog. When in this mental state, we don't like to change. Starting small helps you start making the choices you want without having to also fight yourself.

Like with your exercise, start somewhere that is just slightly outside your current comfort zone. If all you can manage is eating ham and cheese on a tortilla instead of on a white-bread sandwich, then simply do that, and let yourself heal a bit more before incorporating more like spinach or kidney beans. Or, if you're a big eater, make the biggest and most satisfying tortilla you can. While still bearing in mind what we've said earlier, get creative with what you put in it. Salmon, pinto beans and cheese with a sprinkling of lemon juice and parsley? Sure, why not?

Another way you can make things easier on yourself while still maintaining some progress is by reducing the daily dish count. For example, use one cup throughout the day for all your drinking water. If the dishes are too daunting and you need the energy for something else, consider ordering a stack of disposable paper plates and eat your meals off those. While this does mean generating extra waste, paper is still a renewable resource. If using paper plates means you'll have more energy to make healthy meals, and be more likely to do other gentle and caring things for yourself, then that extra waste is completely justified. No one we've ever lost would have wanted us to be so miserable after they're gone. Sometimes the best thing you can possibly do to honor their memory is to keep trying to take care of yourself.

CALLING FOR AID

When my Mom passed, I was lucky enough to still have my dad cooking some meals for me most nights. Just the act of eating was often hard enough, and having him around to make the meal for me made it easier to muster up the energy to take a few bites and keep my body going. Of course, the grief was getting to him too, and on some nights, that would mean I'd be cooking for myself. If you live in a friendly neighborhood, you might turn to your fellow neighbor from across the street and work out a temporary arrangement where they produce healthy, ready-made meals for you.

Even if you don't feel like socializing to that degree, you can still gain help by signing up with a meal service such as Amazon-Fresh, UberEats, Purple Carrot, or Blue Apron. The delivery services would be more expensive than shopping and preparing food yourself, but knowing you can call on these companies on days where things just aren't going your way can help you keep your anxiety in check. Letting others help you in some areas of life such as this can be just what you need to let you direct your energy to other important areas, such as self-motivation.

3

WRITE YOUR FEELINGS DOWN

One of my favorite books from childhood was *Life of Pi*. It's about a young boy who survives a shipwreck, loses his family (his mother, father and brother), and then has to survive being lost at sea on a lifeboat… that he is sharing with a collection of escaped animals from his late father's zoo. One of these animals is a tiger.

This is one of the most extreme situations I can ever imagine a person being in, and most of us won't come anywhere near a level of loss and danger as deep as this. The story is, of course, fictional. However, in this book was an entry from a naval survival guide which read that the most important tool for survival is the mind and, when we're lost or alone with no hope in sight, journaling is one of the best tools for keeping our minds sharp, self-aware, and most importantly, functional.

This immediately struck me as a ring of truth. Ship captains in days of yore would keep a journal, not only to help them keep track of their crew and the general state of their ship, but also to maintain their sanity and self-confidence throughout a smelly, wet, stressful and multi-month voyage. Traveling the world was no picnic when they were stuck with sails and oars.

In the modern age, navigating through grief is no easier. Like a ship in the middle of the sea, we're in a scary and unpredictable voyage with no end in sight. However, just like that sea captain, and just like Pi, you can use journaling as a way to help yourself cope. The benefits are not to be underestimated; if it was possible to distill all the long-term benefits of journaling into a pill or tablet, it'd be regarded as one of the biggest medical advances of our age.

THE BENEFITS

The first and most obvious benefit is improved stress-management. Grief is often accompanied by a sense of helplessness, which can cause great anxiety and despair. The overabundance of stress generated by these feelings greatly increases the risk of complicated grief. However, that is not the end of it. Stress, as we know it, is what happens when our subconscious brain sends out the "fight-or-flight" signal throughout our body. This signal dates back to ancient times, and was evolved to help us protect ourselves when under physical attack. Many of us do not need to worry about physical attacks to the same degree our ancestors did, but our brain still sends out the same signal whenever we encounter something that we consider stressful. This is unhealthy in the modern age because our bodies undergo rigorous changes while that signal is active; our stomach shuts down, our muscles tense up, our breathing rate quickens, and our heart pumps faster. While these are useful changes to have when stressed by a sabertooth tiger, in the modern age it simply means that when we get stressed by work, relationships or grief, our bodies are automatically placing a huge amount of unneeded strain on us to try combat a threat that doesn't exist on the physical level. This can lead to headaches, muscle aches, sleep loss, greater risk of illness, and other symptoms we tend to associate with grief. Stress plays a huge role in how we deal with grief.

However, when we write our experiences down, we force ourselves to put what's happening into coherent sentences. By explaining your own problems to yourself, you build neural pathways in your brain which tell your subconscious that what you're going through can't be resolved through a physical response, but there may be another solution. This results in your subconscious becoming less trigger-happy with its fight-or-flight signal, and reduces the physical wear-and-tear you'd otherwise be experiencing during your grief.

Spending as little as 15-20 minutes journaling each day can be enough to lower your blood pressure and even help your liver function more efficiently (Baikie & Wilhelm, 2005). You might even find your appetite improving after 4 months or less once you begin journaling, as stress may be the reason why you're struggling to eat the way you normally would.

From a psychological point of view, writing sometimes causes us to express perspectives that we'd never considered before during our thinking. This can help avoid misunderstandings, increase self-awareness, find unexpected solutions to problems, and generally let us become more in touch with ourselves.

The reduced stress, overall, is a great help in preventing further deterioration. The reduced strain on our bodies also makes it easier to heal not only physically, but also psychologically. It's easier for your cells to regenerate when your nervous system isn't overworking your muscles, and it's easier to recover psychologically and deal with grief on your own terms when your brain functions aren't constantly being disrupted by feelings of panic, rage or fear.

In the long term, this can lead to faster recovery from further tragedies such as job loss or grave illness. Of course, journaling alone won't cause miracle recoveries, but its usefulness in puzzling out issues and reducing stress cannot be understated. Over time, keeping a journal will prove instrumental in expanding your memory and understanding. If you've ever wanted to sharpen your mind, but haven't found the motivation to learn lately, journaling is also a great tool for that. Remember your days in class. The students who did best in school tended to be the ones who wrote about what they learned in their own words. They kept journals on each subject devoted to interpreting and engaging with the academic material.

When you keep a journal, you're effectively spending time interpreting and engaging with the most compelling subject of all: your own life. No one's marking you or pressurizing you to learn more about yourself and your true place in the world (which isn't necessarily the place people say you should be in), so this journal is simply about getting as much value as you can out of your past and present experiences, so that you may grow and become better at engaging with or discussing what you truly care about.

WHY JOURNALING MIGHT BE ESPECIALLY IMPORTANT FOR YOU

When we're grieving, we often feel the need to tell our story and share it with others. At the same time, however, we may also feel completely alone. Maybe we don't feel like anyone's really listening to us. Maybe they don't have the time, or maybe they just don't have the answers at all. But why should you rely on other people to determine how *you* are feeling? Who better to take care of your broken heart than you?

It can be extremely difficult to explain our losses to another person, even when they are willing to listen, but journaling allows us to explain everything however we want, in whatever order we want. The journal becomes a conversation with yourself and, through this conversation, you help yourself release the burden associated with one's worst memories.

And, because this conversation is effectively always with the same person rather than a group of different people, you'll be more likely to pick up on recurring patterns, leading to potentially life-changing epiphanies. If you have no life-long friend or have trouble talking even to those who know you best, a journal then becomes the perfect instrument in your therapy and self-discovery. Sometimes if you want a job done correctly you need to do it yourself, and your emotional healing is likely the place where that adage is most applicable.

Journaling is also a necessity for picking up the pieces of a scattered mind. Having a history or a self-identity is empowering. When a tragedy happens, it can be easy to forget exactly who we are. After all, our relationships are part of what defines us. So, who are we when a relationship ends? Journaling helps you to rebuild your identity as an individual, as you're now given the opportunity to redefine yourself in a new context. Who am I after this loss? How will I choose to carry on later down the line? These can be difficult questions, but being able to answer them reaffirms who you are after a tragedy, and allows you to remove the more selfish parts of your grief from your emotional trauma.

Through this, you can become more mindful of life around you. Being self-aware regarding your desires can make it easier for you to live in the present while still maintaining a view on the bigger picture. Through this, you can become more confident. When we spend time writing about what we want or exploring why we feel the way we do, we gain greater insights into ourselves that allow us to make better decisions more easily. This is what leads to greater confidence.

Understanding why we feel as we do by spending time writing about it also allows us to process our thoughts and feelings more thoroughly. If you are a sensitive soul, or if your emotions are naturally intense, then diarizing your experiences of grief can definitely help you. When putting pen to paper about your heart, you add a touch of serenity to your turmoil. The brain finds it easier to regulate feelings about anything that it deeply understands. When we deeply understand a person, it becomes easy to regulate feelings of love or hate so that they don't encourage us to behave destructively.

When we deeply understand our own feelings, they feel less intense, even though they're no less present than they were before. This lessened intensity isn't due to numbness or a shutting out, it's simply due to perspective. A two-story house looks big, until you've seen a skyscraper. A village feels crowded, until you've lived in a city. An abusive relationship feels like love, until you encounter compassion. But instead of making our current grief look smaller by placing it beside a bigger one, you simply make your current grief more manageable by placing it beside all the other events of your life, including those times when you were conscious of the pain of others.

TIPS FOR JOURNALING THROUGH GRIEF

The best thing you can do is make sure your journal is convenient, like a small notebook that you can keep in your pocket. If something truly profound strikes you in the middle of the day, you cannot assume that you'll still remember what it was by the time you get to your journal if you keep it at home. By keeping your diary small, you can take it anywhere and note down anything you want as it strikes you.

Next, journaling is best done by hand rather than at a computer, as neural pathways form more effectively in your mind when writing on pen and paper. Save your keyboard and screen for work projects. It doesn't matter if no one can read your handwriting, the only person your journal needs to benefit is you. The next thing you should do is write as quickly as you can. We have a tendency to try to refine or censor ourselves, neither of which is useful when we need to tackle the difficult personal questions of life. Writing quickly helps you put all your feelings down before self-censorship has a chance to even show up.

When you're journaling, you're telling the story that no one else has the time or inclination to hear, and you're telling it to yourself because you know it'll add value to your life in ways that no one else can comprehend.

So, when you write something down, keep your hands going along. When journaling for yourself, do not stop to read back any of your previous lines until you have put down your pen for the day. Do not cross out anything you've written, even if it's because of a spelling mistake. Never cross something out just because you think it sounds odd or because you no longer agree with it. Even if you didn't mean to write it at all, keep it.

Those words are part of you, and crossing them out blocks you from exploring your relationship with them until the underlying issue behind them crops up again. If you write so quickly that you're not even staying on the lines or in the margins anymore, just keep going. The sentences just have to be coherent; that isn't always the same thing as being neat, orderly or grammatically correct. Do not make time to second-guess yourself until after you've written everything down for that day. Simply pour out what is in your heart. When you're writing, journaling is all about getting that maelstrom of thoughts in your noggin down onto some paper.

It isn't about gaining control just yet; it's about being raw and real with yourself. When we deal with our thoughts mentally, we can easily get turned around and go in circles. When dealing with them on the lines of a page, it is much easier to break the cycle and move forward.

Note that your writing doesn't have to be limited to any particular genre. If you want, you're perfectly able to write in song or poetry. Freeform is naturally better, but if having vague guidelines for your syllable counts will help you, then by all means use them. Just remember that syllable counts are comparable to spelling or grammar for the purposes of journaling: a means to an end that should be ditched the moment it gets in the way of self-exploration.

The best things to write about are emotional and provocative memories, but you do not necessarily need to repaint a vivid picture of what went down. A psychological study found that recounting traumatic events, or causes of grief, in expressive or abstract ways brought significantly more calmnessr than trying to recount everything in perfect detail. In fact, those who tried to capture every little detail tended to become more upset, as they'd bog themselves down with a lot of mental clutter that doesn't actually relate to their grief beyond existing at the same time the loss happened.

Write the way that Jackson Pollock, Edvard Munch, or Ernst Kirchner would paint. Don't obsess over minutiae; capture what resonates most strongly with you.

If you wish to take your journaling to the next level, however, write about your experiences in the third person (Stang, 2020). Instead of saying "I" or "me" all the time, try "him" or "her", or "he" or "she". When we write about ourselves in the third person, it becomes easier to see ourselves as a character in a narrative or story. When reading about a character, we like to think about what they're going to do next if they're in a challenging situation, or what they could do better in the future if they recently made a mistake. Getting into that frame of mind where you see yourself in that way can be highly useful. You might even be able to compare your story to ones that have come before; for instance, the classic "Hero's Journey," a story-telling format where a relatable but otherwise ordinary individual is propelled into overcoming adversity and accomplishing extraordinary things after a moment of great loss, tragedy or grief.

The "Hero's Journey," ultimately, eventually peaks after many trials and tribulations with the death or loss of something or someone deeply important to the hero. Luke Skywalker, for instance, lost his aunt and uncle, lost his friend Ben Kenobi, and ultimately lost Han Solo. When he learned that Darth Vader was his father, he also felt that he'd lost the dad he never knew, since suddenly a figure he assumed to have always been good was now vividly dark and terrible in his mind. Learning Vader's true identity and losing Han on the same day was Luke's deepest moment of loss, but that loss wasn't the end.

The "Hero's Journey" continues by allowing the hero to change, adapt, and to try and rectify any previous mistakes. In Luke's case, he rescued Han, he helped resist the regime that hurt his family, he honored Ben's memory by finishing his training, and ultimately, he helped Vader return to being the hero he was meant to be.

The "Hero's Journey" is used to tell stories that are larger than life, but the idea of growth or even redemption after a great tragedy is something nearly universal in the human psyche.

What you endure may make your life feel as if it is burning down around you, but even ash can fertilize the soil for further growth. My mother died, and I could not change that. But I could still grow by honoring her memory. The more I wrote to myself about the pain I was going through, the more I began to understand that this was far from the end. The more I realized I was responsible for my emotions to my mother's death, the more journaling I prioritized.

My writings helped me hold onto all my memories of her as I gradually let go of my grief. Thanks to this, I've been able to get closer to peace and come closer to honoring who she was, rather than mourning what is no longer there. Her body and mind are gone, but after everything I've written about her, I feel as if her spirit is always with me. I've since found greater comfort in my words amidst bittersweet thoughts.

4

MEDITATE

There are many ways to meditate but, when meditating in grief, there are certain rites to be aware of. Before we begin, I want you to imagine a rain cloud. Dark, thick and heavy, it blots out the sun. And there it sits, day after day. A rain cloud does not dissipate until it lets its raindrops loose. Likewise, grief cannot subside if we do not allow ourselves to feel it. While the previous three exercises are all about simplifying grief, this should not be confused with trying to avoid grief or ignore it. Everything so far has been written to help you clear away distractions and clutter so that you can focus on your grief while remaining functional enough to survive. You are a survivor... or at least, you will be.

It is good to honor a person in peace when you're ready to do so. Until then, allowing yourself to experience your pain without self-judging is a way for you to honor your grief. You have a right to cry. As tempting as it may be to keep soldiering on, you do not need to take on the hard heart of a soldier to survive.

To confront your grief through meditation, take a seat. The best place to sit is on a cushion on the floor, cross-legged. The next-best place to sit is on your bed, cross-legged, but only if sitting on your bed doesn't make you feel unusually drowsy. When you're sitting in this way, remove any coverings you have on your face. This includes spectacles and contact lenses. If it's easier for you to meditate in the morning before putting your coverings on, that's fine too.

Wherever you sit, make sure the room is dry and has light pouring into it. Dampness and darkness tend to wear a person down over time, which causes unexplained feelings of depression. Sunlight is the best light, as it promotes vitamin-D, but any bright light will do if you live in a place that sees little sun.

When you are ready, breathe in slowly. Breathe deeply, so that you can feel the air even at the very bottom of your lungs refresh and detoxify. After you have taken a few deep breaths, let your body fall into a natural rhythm of inhalation and exhalation. Do not try to control this rhythm, but maintain your awareness of your breath. Maintain awareness of the feeling in your chest as your lungs fill up with cool, fresh air, and exhale all that is stale. As you're breathing, place your hand on the center-left of your chest, where you can feel your heartbeat. Keep your hand there, but very gently. Imagine your heart is an infant that you need to cradle; touch it reassuringly, keep it safe, but don't become too firm. Do not constrict it. Don't shut it away. Maintain awareness of your breath, and feel your heart as it expands and contracts in your chest.

Next, when you are ready, begin to recall the memories leading up to your event of grief. If you are not ready but wish to continue in some way, you can do so simply by recalling the emotion instead of the events around it.

Keep your hand on your heart, and do not forget about your breath. If you've been journaling, then this may be a little easier. If you're struggling, don't stress. Grief can already be a struggle, so don't let anxiety distract you from it. If your memories are wanting to come forth vividly, let them. Do not shut them out. Let the narrative, the imagery, and the emotions all build up naturally. Do not force anything. Let it come as it does.

Keep breathing, and keep your hand against your heart. Observe what happens as each emotion comes forward. How does your breath feel? How does your heart feel? How does your body react as you experience love? What about anger? Or regret? If your anxiety hasn't left you, do not fret; simply pay attention to what it is doing to your heart and your breath.

Feel your heart gently through each of these emotions, no matter what order they come in or how long they last. Do not rush; give yourself enough time to deal with each feeling as it arrives. Be kind with yourself. You are part of this world, and this grief is now part of the world's grief. If you need to cry, let your tears fall to the ground. If you are outside, let the soil keep your grief. If you are indoors, let your tears hit the carpet, or the floor. From there, let them evaporate into the Earth's air so that it can keep your grief that way instead.

When you are finished, your grief will still be with you, but you may notice that rather than being a dark and all-consuming void, it is now more like an ebony soil. It is fertile, with a potential for growth and life. You do not have to plant anything in there yet, but through allowing yourself to meditate in this way, your grief will not simply be your opponent; it'll become your partner in resolving an even deeper question.

IMPERMANENCE

Nothing lasts forever. The world is in constant flux. In this universe, frogs and salmon are spawning their eggs at the same time that ancient stars are collapsing and new ones emerging. Great cliffs are worn away by the ocean, continents shift on tectonic plates, entire beaches can get carried off and then deposited on the other side of the world. Mighty buildings fall into disrepair when unmaintained, and great wounds heal in time. Philip Ardagh once said, half-cocked, "Time is a great healer... it also gives you the opportunity to bleed" (Ardagh, 2008).

The idea to focus on is that nothing is permanent, things are constantly changing, including our state of wellbeing. Whether it's for better or worse, nothing stays as it is. In a materialist society, focused on accumulating vast stocks of things, people often inadvertently train their minds to see the world as permanent, static, unchanging. However, permanence is merely an ideal that exists only in frozen images or perfect imaginary futures. Permanence does not exist in the present, because when we open our eyes we see new things happening all the time. Even the skin cells on your fingertips are being born and dying at a phenomenal rate. Change, then, is our only constant.

But what does this mean in terms of our grief? Does it mean we shouldn't grieve? Of course not! We have every right to mourn our losses! What impermanence teaches us, however, is that the future is never set in stone and that we aren't perfect, godlike beings with the power to perfectly control outcomes all the time. It also teaches us that *we* aren't as set in stone as we think either. This encourages us to be more mindful of what is happening to us and around us right now, and gives us the freedom to redefine who we are according to our present circumstances rather than who we thought we once were, or who we think we should be. Of course, our actions in the present can influence what happens in the future, but the present is where our true control lies.

What impermanence also teaches us is that our grief won't be the same from day to day either. When we try to imagine a future with our grief, we tend to see it as dark and unending, whereas the truth isn't so bleak. What is true, however, is that we feel dark and unending *now*. But maybe we'll feel okay tomorrow. One day, we might even smile. But then, maybe the very next day, our grief will be back and it'll hurt like hell.

When we accept that our grief isn't a constant in life, but rather an aspect of our present that rises and falls like the ocean, it becomes a little less scary. Thanks to the triggering of the "avoidance" parts of our brain, especially in complicated grief, we often want to try to dance around our own pain, to ignore it, as a way to move on with life. But again, our grief is impermanent. It will come and go as it pleases, regardless of our constant wishes, until it can resolve itself. The best way to work through grief then is not by trying to run away from it, but rather from acknowledging it when we feel its presence, and then *permitting it to leave*. This is gentler than the commonly-held belief that grief must be evicted, as well as being more effective in the sense that this softer stance tends to prevent internal conflicts. Although you may suffer, at least you won't be tearing yourself apart as well. Your grief deserves your attention on its own, it does not need to be partnered with more pains.

Of course, I do not mean to imply that you're running from your own grief in that last paragraph, but such an idea was something I have been tempted by myself, so I wished to assure you that there are other ways through this.

Most of us, I feel, will find it easy to acknowledge our grief when it manifests in us. Usually, the difficulty is in gaining a deeper understanding, or in getting others to acknowledge our pain with us. The greatest difficulty, however, is in letting go. So, how do we do this? Why should we?

LETTING GO

What does it mean to let go? From Chapter 1, you may still remember that it does not mean letting go of memories. It does not mean letting go of love. It means letting go of mental clutter and clearing away distractions, just like before.

Let me show you.

Return back to your meditation position, in your light and dry sitting area. Make sure your spine is supporting your body. This time, place a greater focus on your breathing. Instead of placing your hand on your heart, place it just above your belly button. If you can feel any tension in your muscles, let that tension go but keep your hand where it is. Additionally, make each breath as deep as you can, exercising your diaphragm. Count each of your exhalations as you go. Now, we are primed to let go. The practice of letting go is actually quite easy, and isn't as extreme as one might think. All you need to do is be aware of your thoughts; our minds love to wander, especially when we're breathing or counting. These thoughts could be related to your grief, or they could be related to something unrelated, like your socks.

However, once you grab onto any subject in your mind, your thoughts may begin to spiral. Do I have enough clothes in my cupboard for the coming season? Did I remember to pick up fresh socks to replace the ones that got all those holes in them? Oh, hang on, I'm wearing sandals this month so it shouldn't matter anyway. But wait a second, what if so and so pulls through and they end up making plans for us to cycle together this weekend? Do my cycling shoes still fit me?

Your thoughts, once a subject is in mind, can run potentially forever. Letting go, in the context of grief, simply means recognizing when your thoughts are about to enter a spiral and then, very gently, bringing your focus back to the counting of your breath. The more you practice this, the better you'll become at noticing when your thoughts are spiraling. The better you become at noticing this, the better you'll be at bringing your mind back to a point of focus and concentration. Eventually, you won't even need to meditate to do this; you'll be able to bring your thoughts back to a neutral starting point from anywhere.

This is how you let go. Your grief will never be gone but, by developing a will to return your mind to a neutral point instead of getting lost in a spiral, you will become the master of your pain, rather than letting your pain become the master of you.

This "neutral point" may still feel bittersweet, or tinged with sadness for a while. This is alright. The important thing is that you're able to step back mentally when what you're experiencing begins to spiral into a sensation that feels insurmountable. When you let go and reset for a second, you give yourself a second chance to look at your experience. When you do this, continuing with a meaningful life begins to seem more possible again.

This is because you're giving yourself space to deal with your grief on your own terms. Your grief may seem to come and go according to its own will, but by being able to notice its presence and bring your thoughts back to pace accordingly, you give yourself the ability to tell your grief, "Okay, I think I see what you're saying, but please slow down and start over."

Cutting our spirals short helps us spot what's hurting us most, and from there helps us decide when and how best to address our emotional wounds.

MINDFULNESS

Nothing is permanent. Your emotions, especially, aren't unchanging entities. They aren't absolutes either. Grief is not good. Grief is not bad. Anger is not good. Anger is not bad. It all depends on the context and how you choose to act on what you feel. Even love can become abusive or possessive when it is not matured with compassion, and even compassion can be misleading from time to time when used without experience.

Does this mean it's best to then suppress our emotions so that we never make mistakes or feel pain? Of course not.

Growing up without pains or mistakes is impossible, and grief is not the only thing you are permitted to feel during this time. A nasty side effect of early attempts to suppress or avoid our grief is that we often end up suppressing many of our other emotions too; they all flow through the same medium, after all. Accidentally suppressing your thoughts can stunt your ability to deal with grief, and may even lead to depression. Suppressing thoughts or feelings can also prevent valuable growth from taking place.

For instance, maybe deep down you felt relieved when someone you loved died. Normally, the thought is unthinkable. But what if you'd watched them suffer in great pain fighting illness for the past few months? As sad as you were to see them go, part of you is happy that at least they've found peace. There is no shame in this. Seemingly contrasting feelings are allowed to coexist with one another.

Some people even have the urge to laugh after they've experienced a deep loss because as depressing and senseless as life can be, it is equally absurd. These feelings are often difficult to talk about with those close to us because it's very easy for our words to come out the wrong way. "I'm happy he died," never sounds good, no matter what the actual meaning or intention was. This is partially why I recommended journaling earlier; it helps you discuss things that no one else can really understand. It's also why I recommend meditation to you; it helps you catch thoughts that might at first seem overwhelming or confounding.

It took me a while to realize but, eventually, I learned that the intensity of my grief actually has very little correlation with how much I loved my mother while she was alive. This was difficult to spot at first, because I loved her very much, but also grieved very much as well. It was only as I gradually let go of this pain while holding onto her memory that I began to learn this lesson. It was only as the sadness became distant while my love remained close that I understood. This annoyed me a little, because it would've been a handy thing to know earlier. No matter.

Mindfulness and meditation are important because one's culture isn't a one-size-fits-all solution to how we deal with grief. The point is, giving ourselves time for self-reflection is vital for personal resolution. If we depend too much on outside sources, then we have too many people telling us it is time to move on, or get over it, as though grief was nothing but a 5-foot fence.

Everyone grieves at their own pace. Even now, I still have moments where I cry from my past grief. I look at what I've gone on to accomplish in my personal life, and it makes me sad to think my mother will never see it, or that I'll never know for sure if she sees it.

Grief, particularly grief from death, is one of the most difficult things to live through. Breaking my arm, burning my hand, or even getting sand shot into my eye didn't hurt anywhere near as much. Even acknowledging that you're on one of the most difficult paths of your life can be reassuring. If meditation gives you mindfulness and mastery over this, then you can gain mindfulness or mastery over anything.

5

SLEEP BETTER

HOW GRIEF AFFECTS SLEEP

When we first lose someone important to us, sleep can feel nearly impossible. Our bodies are wired to stay awake during times of stress, and this includes the intense anxiety of complicated grief as well as the low hum of depression.

Though you might be lucky enough to have avoided developing complicated grief, 25% of people who experience bereavement from losing a romantic or marriage partner end up developing clinical depression within the first year of their loss, making sleep even harder.

Even if you are fortunate enough to be part of the remaining 75%, basic grief also comes with trauma that leads to disruptive physical symptoms that can last for months. This in turn can lead to insomnia, even in cases where complicated grief does not develop (Tuck Sleep, 2020).

Common barriers to a restful sleep are constant thoughts of loss, which keeps us stressed especially if we haven't been regularly journaling or exercising. In cases where sleep is achieved, it's still possible to wake up feeling a new intensity of bereavement after dreaming about one's lost loved one. Such dreams are commonly a way for our subconscious minds to process the grief on an emotional level, so do not worry if you are experiencing them; it is a sign that your body is trying to heal itself. It's also a clear sign that you need to give yourself more time to process your trauma.

There is nothing wrong with thinking or dreaming about a lost loved one. However, when we dwell on these thoughts obsessively to the point of losing sleep, we begin to enter a vicious circle.

Sleep deprivation occurs either when we're getting substantially fewer hours of sleep than we're used to, or when we're getting the same–or even more–hours but at a wildly inconsistent pace. Sleep deprivation, in turn, makes us more susceptible to illness as well as reduces our ability to cope with stress and anxiety. This vulnerability to stress and anxiety makes it harder for us to meditate, harder for us to process our grief and harder for us to accurately recall information, harming our ability to think and make effective decisions.

All these issues can then increase the severity of our grief, making it even *harder* for us to sleep, increasing the severity of our sleep deprivation and beginning the grief-intensifying cycle all over again. To get the most out of the previous 4 habits, then, we need to pay special attention to our sleep.

In contrast, how does good sleep affect grief? To start, a good night's sleep significantly reduces the odds of developing complicated grief or depression further down the line and makes any existing depression or complicated grief easier to deal with. A good sleep makes it easier for us to keep our heads clear and deal with our pain on our own terms, but on a more foundational level than meditation. Good sleep is a force multiplier for all your other coping mechanisms and grief-processing habits.

HOW MUCH PRIORITY SHOULD YOU PLACE ON SLEEP?

Many of us make the mistake of thinking sleep isn't important, while some of us simply feel too busy to prioritize it much. As a result, perhaps you wish to puzzle out how big of a difference some extra attention to your sleep will make for you.

Several scientific studies have been carried out to demonstrate how important observation of proper sleep routines are for grievers, especially if they're widows or widowers. Psychiatry research published by Elsevier uncovered that you're 4 times more likely to suffer from sleep deprivation than normal while grieving. This was discovered when 100% of all widow participants were found to suffer from poor sleep compared to only 25% of all non-bereaved participants. If you've lost someone, then, poor sleep may certainly be making things harder than you'd expect (Pasternak *et al*, 1992).

Another study published by Elsevier in 1996 further uncovered that deeper feelings of grief led to more serious levels of sleep deprivation, in line with our earlier idea of sleep deprivation and bereavement forming a vicious circle (Brown *et al*).

For women, the issue can be even worse as both menstruation and menopause can lead to sleep-disrupting changes in body chemistry. It can be especially difficult for older women, as the decreased production of estrogen and progesterone in the Autumn months already leads to risks of depression and sleep loss before grief is even factored in (Tuck Sleep, 2020c).

So, if you are approaching middle-age, are grieving over a death, or are female, then resolving your sleep could lead to a massive improvement to your overall wellbeing.

However, it doesn't stop there; don't think you can ignore sleep just because you're young or male. In a study conducted by Research Gate in 2005, observations of over 800 college students of various ages and genders found that those in mourning exhibited more severe degrees of insomnia and impaired cognition, with the common barriers mentioned earlier being the biggest reasons.

The European Respiratory Journal also found that in cases where the loss was the death of a family member in intensive care, the chances of developing complicated grief rose from 25% to 50%, additionally increasing the chance of poor sleep and the beginning of a truly vicious cycle.

In other words, the more personal your loss, and the more deeply you feel it, the more deeply you'll benefit from giving care to your sleep cycle. However, everyone who grieves will suffer from poor sleep to some degree, and can thus still benefit from the advice below.

CREATING AN IDEAL SLEEP SCHEDULE

When we're grieving, we already feel overwhelmed. Certainly, the thought of sorting out our sleep schedule isn't likely to cross our mind and, even if it does, how do we start?

The golden rule is consistency. If you've ever heard stories of people achieving great success on very little sleep, your jaw may have hit the floor. "How on Earth do they do it?" you may have asked. The trick is consistency. Most people are comfortable with 7-8 hours of sleep per night, although some can run on 6 while others need 10-12. Regardless of how much you need, setting a schedule to both go to bed and to wake up at the same time every day, even on weekends, already kicks you off to a good start. The longer you keep to these times, the easier they'll be to live by, and the better you'll feel. So, right now, go ahead and set a sleep and wake-up time for yourself that you're comfortable with. As with all things, don't be afraid to take baby steps. You don't want your sleep/wake times to be more than an hour more or less than what you're used to. If you want, choose something based on the schedule you had before your grief.

Now that you've decided on a time, you might be asking, "Well, how do I make sure I will stick to this? What if my body doesn't want to sleep when I do? What if my thoughts are too difficult to sleep through?"

Luckily, there are ways to cope and retake control of your rest.

The first thing you may wish to do is cut naps out of your schedule. An afternoon siesta is fine if you're used to it, but for most people, naps only make it harder for them to get the sleep they need at night. To avoid this, it is recommended that you keep your naps no longer than 30 minutes; it can be quite difficult to wake from a sleep that goes on longer than half an hour. If you absolutely must sleep longer than that time, make it no longer than one hour, and set an alarm to make sure you'll get up when you need to.

However, naps aren't exactly our biggest worries, are they? After all, the common barriers to a good rest are tortured dreams and thoughts of loss, not siestas. To help remind yourself that you are not alone, and that you do have love and support should you need it, consider reaching out to a friend or family member. Invite them to spend time with you, and even invite them to spend the night if you'd like. If friends or family aren't available, letting a pet comfort you can also be effective. If you shared a bed with your loved one before your loss, consider sleeping on their side of the bed. You might find it comforting, if still bittersweet, and it might be easier to sleep when you're not constantly looking at the empty space they used to occupy. It might be easier to look at your own empty space. A body pillow can help even further; body pillows not only support your muscles and help them relax, the feeling of holding onto something soft can help your body and mind wind down just enough to get a healthy sleep. The pillow won't replace your lost loved one, of course, but that's not the point of the pillow; the pillow is just there to help you maintain your physical and mental health during a trying time.

The next best thing to do is cut alcohol or sleeping pills out of your pre-bed ritual. While they can be handy for enforcing consistency in your sleep, they don't allow for very deep sleeps, and can even give you terrible bouts of anxiety while you're unconscious, severely limiting your rest quality and causing feelings of fatigue regardless of how many hours you were knocked out. If you absolutely need a sleeping aid, ask your doctor about melatonin supplements. Melatonin is a natural hormone produced by your body when you're in dark or dimly lit areas. The more melatonin in your system at once, the drowsier you become. This hormone is what usually lets us fall asleep, but it's quite common for its natural synthesis to be disrupted by great stress after a loss.

In these cases, getting melatonin can be quite helpful for getting your sleeping cycle back on track, but there are natural alternatives to help bring your melatonin production back to a healthy schedule.

THE NATURAL WAYS

Let's start with the low-hanging fruit; caffeine is not recommended after lunchtime. Caffeine's wakefulness effects can last up to 6 hours after you drink it, and its alertness boost does not necessarily increase awareness; rather, it makes you more anxious and twitchy. Coffee is an obvious source, but most sodas and colas have this issue, as well as some teas and many forms of hot chocolate. Consider these drinks "comfort food," as per Chapter 2. These may have been fine for you in the past when you didn't have grief to contend with, but the wakefulness brought by these drinks is too much when dealing with bereavement simultaneously. Keep these drinks for the morning and afternoon, and stick to water in the evening. Small amounts at night are still fine, but only if you're confident you'll still be able to sleep well. If you aren't sleeping well, these drinks may be a contributing factor to your frustration.

Other than that, the dietary recommendations given in Chapter 2 will already help you achieve more peaceful sleep at night. If you need a little extra help, increase your intake of oats, bananas, tomatoes, walnuts or cherries during dinners or desserts, all of which are rich in natural melatonin.

If you want to boost your body's melatonin production rather than relying on foods already containing it, however, then you may prefer foods rich in vitamin B6. Vitamin B6 helps your nervous system send signals properly throughout your body. This will not only improve your body's ability to produce melatonin when it is needed, but it may also have an added effect of helping you process what's around you and find greater calmness as a result.

Foods rich in B6 include pistachio nuts, bananas, raw garlic, chickpeas and fish. Out of the fish, halibut and tuna are some of the richest in B6, as is salmon.

Aside from your diet, you can also improve your sleep every night through controlling the lights in your house. Remember, melatonin is produced in dim light and darkness. Leaving your lights on, then, just encourages you to stay awake longer.

Note that, although the yellow lights of your house may be the most obviously bright light sources around you, your phone and computer screens are actually much worse. Although they won't brightly light up a room the same way a bulb does, the light emitted by screens tends to be based on blue light. Blue light is by far the most intense kind of visible light, and as such stimulates your brain far more than the yellow light of your bulbs. This stimulation can encourage you to stay awake even after the blue light has been blocked or turned off and, for this reason, it is best if you avoid phone and computer screens as much as possible about an hour before you intend to sleep.

Beyond our body's physical response to screen light encouraging us to stay awake, screens tend to show us a host of mental stimulants that keep us up too; social media is readily addictive and stimulating in its random reward system. Dramatic, explicit or unnerving content can also keep our brain ticking for hours after we turn our screens off, making sleep difficult after watching a horror movie or emotional TV drama. Avoiding these kinds of shows and content for at least an hour before bed can help you get a restful sleep without cutting these things out of your life entirely.

Finally, our digital media can be full of reminders of our loss, which can raise anxiety and encourage unhelpful rumination if we aren't journaling. Of course, it's a bad idea to avoid these things entirely; simply give yourself time to deal with them earlier in the day so that you can leave your nights open to soak in your melatonin and drift off to sleep.

TURN YOUR BEDROOM INTO A SANCTUARY OF SLEEP

Aside from diet and darkness, there are additional ways to gently transform your bedroom into a more comfortable place to sleep. Part of this lies in how you treat your bedroom.

The first thing you may wish to do is locate any reminders of your loved one, like photographs, books or clothing. Although these objects can trigger grief, it's important to spend a little time with them so you can decide what to do with them. If you've been battling to sleep due to grief, consider moving these items to other parts of your house, such as your living room. As a general rule, it's a good idea to keep anything not associated with sleep or sex outside of your bedroom; this will make it easier for your brain to associate your room with sleep and thus get into the correct mood for deep rest. Moving objects associated with your lost loved one to other parts of the house, then, can tell your brain that it's okay to set aside grief at least a little bit in order to achieve a good night's rest. Decluttering other objects like electronics, toys or excess items can further help your brain focus on sleep, even if the items have very little to do with your loved one. You can make the relocation of these items temporary, or until you feel your grief is manageable again. Alternatively, you can choose to relocate these items permanently. It is up to you.

If you have the energy to redecorate your room entirely, strongly consider using shades of blue, which tend to evoke feelings of calm and hope. Even if all feels lost, hope remains a useful tool for overcoming psychologically stressful situations. If your bedroom isn't a quiet place, consider playing electronically recorded sounds taken from nature as ambient noise. Although noise typically disrupts sleep, constant sounds like the wind, the ocean or crickets chirping can loop back to being soothing. Disruptive sounds can ruin our sleep quality even while we're dreaming, but soothing ambiance or complete silence can let us get the quality rest we need during grief.

Another thing you can try to help get into the right mindset for sleeping in your bedroom is the development of a bed-time routine. Pick something you'd be comfortable doing every day about 1 hour or less before bed. An obvious one is to start dimming or even turning off the lights inside your house, and making sure all your curtains are firmly shut, so that it's dark enough for your body to ramp up the melatonin production.

A warm bath or cup of caffeine-free tea (such as herbal or chamomile) are also great ways to help your body relax physically, making sleep an easier prospect. If you find it difficult to get off your electronic devices, despite knowing how bad they are for your sleep, consider writing letters or reading a book instead as a way to unwind without exposing yourself to blue light. Finally, consider meditating before bed, just like how we described in Chapter 4. Meditation will allow you to bring today's grief forward and deal with it compassionately, allowing you to resolve some of your pains so you don't carry them all to bed.

SYNERGIZING EXERCISE AND JOURNALING WITH SLEEP

Meditation and diet aren't the only tips that synergize with your sleep. When grieving, it is not uncommon to experience restlessness. When waking up in the middle of the night, do not stress, and do not begin watching your clock. Clock-watching is a notorious stressor, and as such will only make it more difficult for you to return to sleep. Rather, if you've woken up, the best thing you can do is just try to fall asleep again, without stressing over how much time it feels like it's taking. Our perception of time isn't always accurate in the middle of the night. Count to 600 while you wait. If you get to 601 and still don't feel sleepy, get up, grab your journal, move into another room and spend a little time writing about your thoughts. Writing about what's bothering you can help you process it just enough so you can comfortably return to bed again.

You are welcome to re-enact your bedtime routine of tea, bathing or reading again if you wish, and then once again return to bed. Giving yourself some time to unwind in this way during a restless night can help you make the most of what time you have left.

Exercising in the evening after you are finished with work can also help tire your body out further and put it in the mood to rest, which can help with sleep. Do not do this less than an hour or two before bed, however, as the energy activated by your exercise will need some time to cool off before its drowsiness effect will kick in. If you have less than 60 minutes before bed, or if you've woken up in the middle of the night, it is better to stretch than to perform full-on exercises so that you avoid activating your energy stores, which could potentially keep you up much longer than you intended if timed poorly.

6

UPDATE YOUR BRAIN

In Chapter 2, I compared the human brain to a computer and stated that water was the coolant needed to keep it running optimally. So far, we've largely been dealing with "hardware": how to take care of your body, and how to reduce physical and emotional stress on a mechanical level. However, your hardware is only one side of boosting performance. To run as best you can, you also need updated software.

Software updates help eliminate bugs or block viruses. Likewise, updating your brain helps you spot limiting beliefs, remove logical fallacies and block misleading or self-destructive thoughts.

But how do we update our brains? By reading, of course!

If you've been struggling to make time for reading, choose a book on something you enjoy; books these days cover everything from culture, science and religion to fantasy, comedy and legend. Once you've chosen something compelling, make a point of reading anywhere between 1-40 pages from that book each night as part of your pre-bed routine. If you use public transport, another great reading spot is on the bus or train. Finally, if you're so absolutely busy that neither of those options is viable, at least keep it for your lunch breaks. Some people speak as if TV and books are mutually exclusive, but this does not need to be true.

But, thanks to the benefits, it's recommended you fit reading at least somewhere in your life. If I've done my job, you've already updated your brain several times as a result of what you've read so far. Just like journaling, reading is a powerful self-education tool that can empower you through opening new doors and considering new perspectives.

EMPATHY AND PERSPECTIVE

Speaking of perspective, reading is a doorway into the minds of other people. This means that the stereotype of the arrogant and insufferable bookwork is not inherently true; while reading very narrowly can cause tensions, it is also true that reading widely allows you to broaden your mind and, through understanding, become a more compassionate person. By reading this book, for instance, you have been given a key into parts of my mind, and through that the opportunity to grow closer to me as a person, even though we may have never met. We all live through our personal narratives and have our view of the world subjectively distorted through our experiences, and allowing me to share mine with you is a treasure that benefits us both.

However, no single person's experiences lend a complete view of life. Reading is what lets us see into the minds, motivations, insights and value systems of people from other cultures, faiths, age groups, gender identities, sexualities, economic classes, and more. Reading, then, is not just a source of knowledge and ideas, it is also a way for us to understand other people in this world. Reading also gives us the rare gift of allowing us to see into people's minds across centuries. Even in a world where nothing is permanent, what a person writes tends to outlive the person themselves, giving us insights into how humans from a variety of cultures lived, spoke and thought.

When we're grieving, reading about someone else's trials and tribulations can sometimes feel like the last thing we want, and yet it's those alternate perspectives that we come to crave when we feel lost. After all, that's why you're here, isn't it? Whether a book is fictional or not, reading about another person's experiences and how they overcome the obstacles in their life is, when written well, inspiring. It makes our own obstacles seem more possible. An uphill battle that once seemed hopeless now looks winnable. The best fantasy and science fiction works not because it's full of wizards or space-giants or enchanted laser swords. The best science fiction and fantasy stories work because the main characters are still relatable on a very grounded level, and their ability to learn about, navigate and cope in such a strange world is encouraging. Real life itself is quite strange, too.

As difficult as it was for me to lose my mother in such a short amount of time, Joan Didion's *The Year Of Magical Thinking* gave me solace and perspective; she'd lost her husband at the same time that her daughter was in a coma, and she dives into the events in a raw biography of beauty and pain. Reading it inspired me to soldier on and find new hope. Any genre in both fictional and non-fictional storytelling can help with grief if it is sensitive, observant and well-written. Never forget that.

Reading widely, from authors of many different viewpoints and creeds, will let you inhabit multiple perspectives at a time. This way of seeing things will make it easier for you to understand multiple angles on any given issue, but also the thought processes of those around you. The more thought processes you encounter through reading, the more likely you are to respond compassionately to the thought processes of others, because you'll be more likely to relate them to an author or character you familiarized yourself with in the past.

This in turn can lead to you forming more deep and complex relationships, as long as you recognize that a person is more than the thought processes they choose to show; who they remind you of isn't all they are, by any means. But being able to engage with what they present to you on their surface is what will help you engage more deeply further down the line. This can reduce loneliness, strengthen existing connections, and give you a powerful web of support in times of grief. Empathy is one of the most powerful social skills on Earth, and mind-reading is one of the most awesome superpowers. Reading widely and frequently will help you develop the first, and get awfully close to mimicking the second.

Finally, reading can cut down your insomnia by half, dramatically increasing the quality of your rest and, consequently, reducing the odds of lashing out or being irritable with those around you. This, in turn, can help you establish greater levels of empathy before even factoring your multiple perspectives into account.

STRENGTHENING INNOVATION

Being able to consider a subject from multiple perspectives isn't just to improve empathy or simulate mind-reading, however. When you constantly expose yourself to the ideas of other people, you begin to see patterns and form connections between their work that allows you to develop their thoughts along a path that even they might never have expected. This is how inventions and advancements are made. Being familiar with one person's work will only let you understand that specific artist, but being familiar with many people's works and seeing where they could potentially support each other can let you create something novel and new. We are not finished inventing everything yet; most of us simply don't read enough to conceive of anything new.

And that is just in the context of non-fiction. In the realms of fiction, a good book will encourage us to visualize detailed characters and grand vistas in our minds. Unlike films, which tend to spoon-feed us both audibly and visually, books let our imaginations become virtually limitless in the way we interpret words and shift their contexts. Reading, then, turns you into your own virtual filmmaker, crafting dozens or even scores of different scenes rolling in your mind, possibly all focused around a single paragraph.

This encouragement of the imagination is good for your brain for reasons similar to why journaling is; it makes you an active interpreter and creator who is involved in the information being presented. Any piece of media that succeeds at this is brilliant, but books are encouraged the most to get this aspect right. A film or video-game can afford to cut their budget on the writing if the visuals, mechanics or acting are good enough, but a book cannot afford a cop-out like that. Writing is all a book has, and for this reason, a greater proportion of published books are likely to contain ideas primed to spark your creative side compared to the number of published films or games.

If you ever feel stuck or unsure what to do next, reading multiple books on the subject will invariably inspire you and give you more creative wiggle room to achieve the kind of life you want.

And, as you read, you'll begin to realize more and more how little any of us truly know. The more you read the more you'll naturally want to make time for reading, as your thirst for knowledge will only grow. This knowledge will continue to empower you in unexpected ways, in turn. Intelligence isn't something we're just born with, it's something we earn through experience; a person who doesn't read will only ever have their own experiences, but the person who reads and forms connections between everything they learn will accrue the experience of a thousand lifetimes, and consequently endow themselves with a wisdom that far surpasses their years. If you're worried about becoming haughty in your knowledge, simply remember that what you learned did not start with you; what you have is a gift that's been built on by people around the world across chasms of time.

ANALYTICAL THINKING

The benefits of reading do not just end at vicariously living multiple lives or benefitting from the enhanced generation of ideas, however. Reading not only stimulates the creative side of your brain, but encourages your logical side too. While you can analyze any book, including fictional ones if they're well-written, Western Nonfiction books especially present us with a body of information that was structured with intention in a specific order. Getting into the habit of critically analyzing the order that books present their information in, and even challenging the established order through seeing where else a paragraph or chapter could fit, will greatly enhance your ability to organize information rationally. After doing this with many books, the process will become quick, easy and natural.

You can take this a step further by trying to map out a summary of the book's narrative on one page. Schools tend to make the process feel boring and dry, but it's actually a wonderful way of taking your depth of analysis to the next level, as spotting and ordering narrative elements according to your own observations can help you pick up patterns you may have missed. You might even spot arcs and themes you'd missed before. Just bear in mind that almost anything can be made a theme with enough creativity; logical analysis, however, is what lets you consider the merit of a theme beyond its premise.

In the modern-day, you can take your analysis even further by using websites like TVTropes, which tend to be amazing starting points for those who want to broaden their analysis or spot overlooked threads in a story. Although, in the same way that a book club won't necessarily help you write a book, sites and forums similar to TVTropes can only encourage a certain form of logical analysis; it's good for breaking down a piece of work. Creating a work, however, requires imagination (see previous section).

FORMING CONNECTIONS

Becoming knowledgeable of alternate perspectives and building empathy already helps one with forming connections, but what are the other ways in which writing aids such endeavors? After all, surely it isn't possible to read a book by every sort of person on Earth? How can reading possibly help with forming connections on a universal level?

Even if you do not understand a particular person's point of view, being a widely-read individual at least increases the chance of there being some common ground or overlap.

When you have read the same book as another person, you immediately have a strong building-point for a friendship. This person can then provide you their perspective in a fun manner if you then decide to unpack the book's contents together. I do this with one of my best friend's, and the conversations we have are some of the most in-depth I've had in my life, I'm sure he'd say the same.

But even if the people you're dealing with have not read the same books as you, and you do not understand their perspectives, your expanded vocabulary gained through reading can increase the chances of them understanding yours. The more words you know, the more easily you'll be able to approach a topic verbally while achieving the result you want. A great example of this is Desdemona's speech to her father in *Othello*, where her use of wordplay allows her to communicate her love for Othello without denouncing or estranging her father. The better our grasp of language and the better our understanding of a word's colloquial use, the better positioned we are to combine context as well as language content to communicate vivid messages. One of Terry Pratchett's great strengths as a writer was his ability to place normally unrelated words alongside one another in ways that people could still readily understand and even appreciate. Being an avid reader improves one's ability to do this through writing, and with a little practice, through speech, with poetry being the logical conclusion of this practice... even though poetry seems to be a somewhat esoteric art in the modern age.

This expanded vocabulary is better for more than just sounding clever or having a wider toolbelt for your verbal communication, however. A heightened understanding of your language, combined with enhanced analytical, creative, and personal empathic skills, can make you an extremely interesting person. That's not to say you aren't interesting already, of course, but sharpening both halves of your brain as well as improving your ability to communicate can help others *see and hear* how interesting you truly are. Not everyone will be interested in the same things of course, but spending time reading what you care about each day will help you come across as more interesting to the kind of people you'd want to hang out with.

Maybe you felt mildly offended when I mentioned the halves of the brain, and believe that the divisions are much more complex than one half being logical and one half being creative. Well, by being well-read on the subject you could launch into a highly-detailed, informative and superlatively interesting discussion on the matter; a discussion you might balk, hesitate or stumble over if you hadn't read enough to feel sure of what you're saying.

And that's another thing; reading makes you more confident in specific areas of knowledge. You might still feel scared, unsure or otherwise lost when it comes to subjects you're not familiar with. A stereotypical computer geek, for instance, might still feel a little uneasy talking about football. But that same geek will be able to reveal an entire world in the micrometer-thick lattices that splay in geometric patterns across your motherboard.

Being able to boast immense self-confidence on certain subjects due to a mixture of knowledge and experience is empowering, although one should never forget that knowledge doesn't just come from books, it comes from people too. When making a real-life comparison to someone who has a mixture of knowledge, I think of Joe Rogan. Listening to his podcasts and the wide variety of guests he has on the show, he asks very thought-provoking questions, while giving his own viewpoint. His ability to hold long conversations with people from completely opposite industries is what makes his show so impressive and popular.

7

CONFIDE

Sometimes, confiding in another person is one of the hardest things we can do. We all want to share our pains with someone close to us, someone who understands, yet often we're held back by fears or disappointment. Maybe the person we're speaking to doesn't understand. Maybe they do, but we feel like we're being a burden. Or maybe there's something we desperately want to get off our chests, and yet we do not have the words. Maybe we just don't feel ready to properly confront what we're going through, even though we feel ready to talk about it. These feelings are all normal; that means as painful as they are, you aren't alone in your experience of them.

The last six chapters were all devoted to helping you take the best care of yourself possible so that the need to confide wouldn't be as strong. In the case of Chapters 3 and 6, you were given ways to help you express your thoughts to those around you without making yourself dependent on their responses.

Now, however, you are ready to start reaching out to others if you haven't already. If you don't feel ready yet, that's alright; you must go at your own pace. Simply know that you're already armed with everything you need to confide in another person once again.

However, friends and family won't always be the people you wish to confide in. While they generally mean well and have your best interests at heart, they also have their own fears and pains to worry about, which means that you might not be able to have as much of their attention as you would like.

If you're ready to confide and yet still feel lonely or unheard despite speaking up, the best thing you can do is seek professional help. Media stereotypes like to portray professional help as a shameful last resort only taken when there is no other choice. This, however, is only because sitcoms with functional individuals aren't as interesting as TV shows where everything is dramatic and blown out of proportion.

Professional help isn't a sign of trouble, or an admission of defeat. Therapists, after all, are simply human beings like you and I. There is no shame in speaking to one. The biggest difference between them and us is that they devote their entire life to helping people conquer grief, overcome fear and achieve resolutions for complex decisions.

It doesn't matter if the troubles are big or small, they are there to listen to you and guide you towards making decisions that ultimately benefit you. Unlike friends or family, who can have their attention divided by their jobs, for therapists this care *is* their job. This, along with professional training in empathy and communication, makes them perfect for helping you scratch long-term psychological itches; family and friends will touch your heart and lift your spirits, but therapists are vital for helping you make psychological breakthroughs that multiply the effectiveness of any compassion shown by your loved ones. For this reason, therapists should not be eschewed. They're like an omnibus of information relevant to your neuroses, so why not pay to read one?

Compare them to dentists; you don't wait until a tooth needs to be pulled before you go and see them, although they certainly are helpful for that. Rather, you visit them somewhat regularly, even if it's just twice a year, and incorporate their advice into your life as much as healthily possible. Likewise, professional therapy is useful even when nothing is particularly wrong. For instance, professional counseling can help reduce the physical harm caused by stress even further, as well as reconnect with your earlier passions maturely.

This reconnection is important, as a lot of what made us special as children is tarnished as we form a series of defense mechanisms in an attempt to protect ourselves from fear, hurt, trouble or any number of suppressive emotions. Therapists have a talent for deftly pointing out recurring thought patterns that may be holding us back in this way, and can help us drop the behaviors that no longer serve our own best interests.

Self-destructive behavior can be subtle, but having it be revealed to oneself can help us escape perpetual feelings of persecution, victimization and powerlessness. Even if we live in a reality where we are persecuted, victimized or disempowered, the insights of a therapist can allow you to find fonts of hidden strength within yourself, and from there help you empower yourself and perhaps even change the reality you live in.

REDEFINE UNHEALTHY PATTERNS

You already have the power to redefine some of your less healthy or grief-amplifying habits, if you have any. Maybe exercise has made it easier for you to cut down on alcohol. Maybe journaling or reading has helped you cut down on other grief-amplifiers, like gluttony or sugar. Certainly, a reading habit is one of the most healthy habits you can have, as binging a book in a moment of weakness is significantly healthier than satisfying that weakness with a cigarettes, a bottle of liquor, or a week's supply of doughnuts.

You already have the power to sort out much of your own confusion and turmoil but, even so, a therapist can be a welcome companion. The habits from the previous chapters allow you to approach your counselor from a position of relative strength, but that doesn't mean you need to pretend as if you have no vulnerabilities at all.

Expressing yourself openly and honestly to someone knowledgeable in the science of therapy can lead to unexpected revelations. One such man, named Eric Hotchandani, found that most of his clients experience a sort of mid-decade crisis every 10 years, where they feel as though they aren't active participants in their own lives. This can lead to expressions of dissatisfaction with relationships, or even their lives as a whole.

According to Eric, this dissatisfaction with life or relations often doesn't have much to do with the relations themselves. According to him, it mostly comes from the common Western practice of filling our houses and lives with objects that aren't personally fulfilling (Tartakovsky, 2019). This doesn't mean that one needs to become a full-blown minimalist to be happy, of course, but he does have a point. By filling our houses with things that don't add value to our lives, we rob ourselves of space and force ourselves into a claustrophobic living environment that leaves us unhappy without adding any corresponding benefit. Living in a dirty or cluttered space can be stressful, and stress, in turn, can exacerbate grief or depression. It's difficult to feel calm when we feel like we're going to be buried under the weight of everything around us.

Even emotional clutter, like the constant belief that we need to be perfect and successful all the time, can be sources of stress that lead to dissatisfaction, even when what we already have is rather good.

When we choose to fill our lives with objects or ideals that do not match our true beliefs or active goals, we end up over-complicating our identities as well as our sense of purpose. In the same way that loss can upset our sense of self, so can possession.

If you aren't a big reader, for instance, owning multiple book-shelves crammed with knowledge that you'll never read can confuse your identity and make you feel like a fraud, even though in reality you may be a deeply intelligent individual thanks to prior learning or strong empathy.

When we continue to keep objects in our lives that aren't in line with who we are, those feelings of confusion begin to become habits. These habits, in turn, become thought patterns that can quickly grow to become a part of one's personality. By this point, the confusion has now seeped into our very identity.

When this happens, we begin to form feelings of self-loathing, most commonly either the feeling that we deserve to live in the bad situation that we're in, or simply that we're not good enough for any of the things that we want in life. We need to remind ourselves that that's simply not true.

Despite this, such feelings invariably leak into our relationships and begin to make us psychologically harm not only ourselves, but also the people we love. Thus, it is important to have such feelings rooted out and addressed. This doesn't mean you can't accept yourself for who you are, but rather it means you are entitled to learn more about yourself and what you can bring into your life to synergize with who you are at your core. When you know how best to meet your core self in the world around you, you'll also know how best to add value back into the place you live.

RELOCATE DESIRE

Desire is not an inherently bad thing. While desire can motivate us to hurt others, or cause us to meddle in places where we shouldn't, this tends to happen when we're not thinking things through. A well-thought-out desire, on the other hand, can be a potent motive that drives us through life, such as the desire to raise a family, or the desire to master a craft.

I compared therapists to books earlier, and for good reason. A decent therapist tends to remind us that our current way of life isn't the only way that we could be living. A good therapist, like a good book, can offer us a broader perspective and deeper awareness, even though it is their empathy that carries this investigation into the self.

It's quite common for individuals to choose isolation as a response to trauma in their lives, and the reasons are ones we can readily understand; we fear opening ourselves up to give to the world only to be rejected. We fear the consequences of placing ourselves in a potentially vulnerable space where we can feel shamed or mocked. And, most of all, we deeply fear the inevitable loss that threatens us when we connect ourselves to another person.

When grieving, that fear of loss becomes fresh in our minds. When we try to share our pain with another person only for their response to brush us off (whether intentionally or not), we can feel rejected. And, most of all, we feel ashamed and mocked when people put us under constant pressure to "get over it" as if they expect our pains to run on their timetable. This shame can make us feel selfish when we are, in fact, just trying to heal from one of the most difficult experiences in our lives. I'd counter that anyone who insists that you "get over it" without actually helping you do so is being selfish themselves.

With all this in mind, it's no wonder that we might wish to isolate ourselves from everyone, especially during or after deep grief. Yet a professional therapist will quickly point out that isolation isn't the final solution for most of us; as much as we fear shame, rejection and loss, most of us also have a deep-seated need for connection.

Even the nerdiest and most anti-social among us need at least 1 or 2 high-quality friends to help brighten up their lives. Despite this, our need for intimacy, whether platonic or romantic, often does not register as a valid desire. In truth, it's one of the most valid desires a person can have. According to the Survivalist's Rule of Threes, a human needs air, water, shelter, food and *love* (The Survival Journal Editorial Staff, 2020). Remember all those funny "stranded islander" characters you'd see in kids' movies? The ones that put googly eyes on coconuts and pretended they're people? As ridiculous as that image is, it is based in truth; no one wants to feel completely alone. And if isolation goes on too long (e.g. a quarter of a year without seeing or hearing another human being at all, perhaps longer if humans are visible or audible but not interactable), the mind begins to do strange things to compensate.

While loss, shame and rejection are all forms of suffering, isolation doesn't prevent that suffering. Isolation instead has us suffer differently because while we might not know the grief of loss again, we instead begin to grieve through having a lonely heart, and the lack of contact invariably leads to chronic depression (see Chapter 1 for symptoms). A therapist can help prevent this by letting you realize and pursue your need for connection in the healthiest manner possible. Isolation does not keep you safe from anything except contagious diseases, and grief is not a disease, nor is depression contagious.

For these things, isolation is not a protective wall, nor is it a secure fortress. In fact, for psychological matters it is best compared to shutting one's eyes to block out the sun, or sticking one's head in the sand in the hope of going unnoticed by one's problems. A grief counselor, then, isn't a siege-breaker. Rather, they are a doctor with earbuds and eye drops, or a rescue serviceman prepared to gently get your head above ground again.

BUT WHAT IS GRIEF COUNSELING, EXACTLY?

As said before, therapy is for any level of grief, and while many of us are grieving from the loss of death, any form of loss can be a cause for grief. Losses such as divorce or estrangement can hit hard, even if it isn't the same thing as death. The pain of grief, meanwhile, isn't simply sadness; it can be anger too.

Therapy, or counseling, exists as both a way to promote understanding of your own grief and a way to help you avoid self-destructive psychological traps while working through your pains. This aid goes above and beyond the advice given in previous chapters, and can be a lifesaver if you were already experiencing great levels of stress or unhappiness before your loss.

A good therapist will commonly get the ball rolling by letting you talk as much as you want about your lost love; they will ask you questions to help you fill their heads with a clear image. They want to understand exactly who and what you lost. During this time, they will withhold on making any judgments and patiently allow you to talk your way through your pains.

From there, the therapist will eventually be able to identify the breaking point between the trauma of your loss and the grief of your loss. A telltale sign that you're undergoing great trauma from loss is if you have an image or memory related to the loss branded indelibly in your mind's eye. The therapist will then identify that, as long as you're undergoing trauma, you'll find processing your grief to be a constant struggle. Their goal from this point is to help soothe your trauma so you can focus on dealing with your grief appropriately. Journaling, as discussed in Chapter 3, might play a part in this, as writing about our experiences lets us bypass the circular ruminations associated with trauma. The therapist, of course, will have further tricks and skills to take this a step further. If journaling hasn't helped you, counseling may be an especially good idea for you.

Trauma usually takes sixteen sessions or more to resolve, though any of the habits you may have picked up earlier in the book can help you get through trauma faster as they help you stabilize, narrate and consolidate your experiences, all of which are needed for effective trauma dissolution.

Finally, a good therapist or counselor will help you identify your guilts and regrets. Perhaps you were skeptical earlier when I mentioned that feeling a measure of relief after a loss is not only common, but acceptable–even if those around you might not understand that. A good therapist will tell you the same thing; there's no "sadness quota" that you need to fill, and what's done is done. You cannot go back and change the past, but you can decide how you'll act going forward. A good therapist, then, will encourage you to let go of the guilt while doing the best you can to honor the memory of your lost loved ones. You could see honoring their memory as a form of atonement, but when done well, it can also become a healthy way of developing your life.

Professional therapists are incredibly well-read, highly educated individuals who deliberately train their empathy, and this leads to a curious set of behaviors. When confessing our pains to others, a common mistake non-therapists make is they open with saying "Oh well, at least <insert minor positive that resulted from a major tragedy>." Even if what they're saying is true, it isn't necessarily what you need to hear. A therapist, meanwhile, will instead respond with another, more helpful truth, "I understand what you're feeling, and I'm here to help you."

A therapist will recall their own instances of pain and grief in their lives, yet very rarely will they share them; this is because your sessions with them are about your pain, not theirs, and that's where they want to keep the focus. Instead, when they're recalling their own pains, they'll ask "What did I wish people told me when I was going through something like this?" or, "If this person is quite different from me, what's the best way for me to help them feel the way I wanted to?"

To figure these things out, a therapist will spend much more time listening to you instead of responding, in contrast to many of the people we try to talk to. They'll also offer you multiple perspectives to consider, and observe you carefully to see which ones you respond to best. For instance, the idea of the 5 Stages of Grief–Denial, Anger, Bargaining, Depression and Acceptance–is actually a severely limited way for people to process their own grief. Yet, because of how popular the format is, people end up putting a lot of pressure on themselves and feel like they're off-kilter if they skipped Bargaining, or experienced Depression both before and after Denial.

This is madness, however, and a good therapist will quickly point that out. After all, the 5 Stages *were originally intended to help individuals anticipate their own deaths.* In other words, they're designed to help people cope with a loss before it happens, but has next-to-nothing to do with processing grief after we live through experiencing a loss. A good therapist, then, will offer other ways of looking at grief-processing. Everyone's grieving format is a little different, and the therapist's ability to determine which format is best for a particular individual is what makes them so valuable.

Now, they aren't necessarily there to solve your problems directly, but they will use truth and understanding to validate how you feel so that you can process things properly yourself.

8

CHERISH POSITIVITY, ACCEPT NEGATIVITY

A s useful as therapists are, however, they are psychological mercenaries. They can thus supplement or even multiply the value of friendships, but they cannot replace them. Your therapist is a learned and attentive companion, but a friend is a friend for free.

That bond of freely given love and companionship cannot be substituted by even the best therapists in the world, despite how useful therapists may be.

For this reason, one of the best habits you can have, both while you're grieving and while you're not, is the cultivation of friendship.

To cultivate the relationships you want, take a moment to consider energy. Have you ever walked into a room only to be instantly hit with a particular vibe? You may think that it's just your imagination, but it's actually your mind picking up on a wide array of subtle cues that then leave an impression. Consider the energy that you like, and consider the kinds of energy that make you uncomfortable.

Take a moment to consider what kind of energy you wish to attract into your life. Now, take a moment to consider what kind of energy you're giving off. Journaling in the third person may help with this if you haven't tried it already. Now, I've heard people say that opposites attract, but that's only for magnets. You and I, we are not magnets; we are human beings.

Like it or not, the energy you give off is the energy you're going to receive right back. Behave in an abrasive manner, even unintentionally, and people will behave abrasively towards you. Put yourself down all the time, and people will begin to put you down too (unless they're keeping track of all the good you do in the world). Sometimes, a handful of nasty people will treat us badly without provocation, but when we give in and use that as an excuse to behave in negative or self-defeating manners, then we will be treated badly consistently by all but the most compassionate of beings.

This is important to note because energy is recursive; the top five people you keep closest in your life will eventually become the top five people you are most similar to. If you surround yourself with positive people, spend time with them, get to know them, discuss their values, then you too will become more of a positive person. However, "positive" is a bit of a vague term on its own, isn't it?

DEFINING YOUR POSITIVITY

Take a moment to write down the names of your top five friends. These friends can include your partner or spouse, or even people from your family. If you don't feel as if you have many friends, just pick the top five people to whom you relate the most.

Now that you have five names down, take time to write down their good qualities; the things you like, appreciate, or even admire in them. Are they funny? Compassionate? Forgiving? Content? Sensible? Exciting?

Think of how they share these qualities with you. Do these qualities make you feel supported or cared for? Do they make you feel that you're growing, or getting closer to what matters to you in life? Do they make you feel like someone worthy of love? Do you feel secure in your relationship with them? Do you tend to feel content or exhilarated after spending time with them?

If you could answer "yes" to even a few of these, then you're likely already surrounded by the kind of people you need in your life, and you can define your own positivity through examining how they behave.

If you answered "no" to too many of those questions, however, then you may need to consider that you have not yet met everyone who is going to make an impact on your life. If you discover that a relationship has been toxic for you, do not become angry with your friend or lover. Do not actively shun them or cast them out.

We are all different from one another. What makes us happy, what supports us, and what drives us won't always be the same. If a person doesn't make you feel worthy of love, secure or content, that doesn't necessarily mean they're a bad person. Usually, it just means that there's a disconnect in communication that needs to be resolved, and it's fully possible to work your way towards resolving such issues and turning a potentially toxic relationship into a happy and fulfilling one, even if a little counseling is needed.

There's no inherent need to cast out the people who are already around you, but if you find that there are gaps in your emotional needs that need filling, do not be afraid to go out and meet more people, or even switch up the way you spend time with people. Do not be afraid to reach out to people you already know in case of hidden depths, either.

When choosing to develop an existing relationship or start a new one, the best thing you can be is forgiving. Holding onto past faults only breeds resentment, which can turn even the sweetest of bonds into a bitter sauce of strife. Creating resentment can also blind you to your own faults, or cause you to act out against your faults aggressively or destructively, which only causes stunted growth and prolonged grief. When you practice forgiving those around you, don't forget to also practice forgiving yourself. This isn't an excuse for you to do bad things, but rather the acceptance that no one on this Earth is perfect and that, as long as we're alive, we have the opportunity to do better.

To do better, strive to be the kind of person you'd want to meet. This is important as people are attracted to those who are similar to them, but with some unique flair. This unique flair is already part of you; no one else has experienced the exact same combination of successes, failures, development arcs, and perspectives as you.

Focus on developing the parts of you that you wish to see in other people, then you will naturally attract other people with those qualities. You might even surprise yourself by bringing out these qualities in someone you already know. However, you cannot bring out a quality that isn't already there under the surface somewhere, so don't aim to change people; rather, aim to discover what they're willing to share with you.

When you make an effort to discover the qualities you value in those around you, whether they're present in your closest family or briefest acquaintances, you'll naturally feel more in love with life. You may even find yourself naturally letting go of minor anxieties and finding joy even in small things. Not everyone who has these good qualities in your life needs to become someone super-close to you, but by making time to interact with them, you'll naturally create a network that supports you, the way a current of wind effortlessly supports a feather mid-air.

WHY WE NEED POSITIVE PEOPLE IN OUR LIVES

As stated before, we tend to become a mixture of the five people we spend the most time interacting with. This means that by making time for positive individuals we help to erode the negative inner voices we may have.

When one's negative thoughts hold a majority in one's mind, we dehydrate ourselves on a psychological level. Remember those thought-spirals we discussed in Chapter 4? When your thinking is negative, you'll be more naturally inclined to spiral negatively.

This can transform a minor annoyance into a seemingly insurmountable problem. This is what leads us to make mountains out of molehills, or to turn a slightly stressful situation into an inescapable nightmare. This negativity, in turn, can cause us to react more aggressively to minor issues, like yelling at a loved one for being unable to teleport. Even though we know they can't bend space and time and appear before us the instant we ask, negative stress-spirals can make us impatient, potentially even beyond reason. This kind of behavior can make it difficult for those you love to grow close to you, as they'll constantly be wondering what little thing will set you off. Meanwhile, you won't be happy either, because your life will feel like an endless stream of one impossible problem after another. The fact that you manage to resolve most of these "impossible" problems will rarely occur to you, because you'll feel so overwhelmed.

Having a supportive group of friends, then, can encourage you to spiral positively instead, or at least prevent you from spiraling too deep into the negative.

This, in turn, can encourage you to think more optimistically. While it's true that excessive optimism can cause a person to waltz into situations woefully underprepared, excessive pessimism is just as bad. When pessimistic inner voices hold a majority in your head, you begin to develop a pessimistic worldview. While the overly-optimistic individual might walk into a scenario underprepared, an overly-pessimistic individual will not walk into a scenario at all, even when they have more than enough to succeed.

Overly-pessimistic people are less likely to recognize their strengths, as well as less likely to recognize when that strength can be used to gain advantages or pursue opportunities. Ironically, this behavior causes the pessimist to fail where they otherwise would have triumphed, reinforcing their negative worldview while keeping them away from their full potential.

A group of supportive friends, therefore, can help motivate you to be the best person you can be, and act as centers of calm in times of stress.

They can help you recognize the positive qualities that you have, even when you weren't aware of them. The best friends tend to pick you up when they know you're down, be playful when they know you're up, and give clear advice when they know you're confused. They won't do this perfectly, of course, but more often or not that's how it will feel when a friend's qualities match up with what you value.

HAPPINESS IS NOT INHERENTLY POSITIVE

At this point, it is important to make a distinction with happiness and positivity, since most of us tend to use the two words interchangeably. Happiness is merely an emotion. Not only that, but it's also a rather fleeting one. Happiness is an intense form of contentment, in the same way that grief is an intense form of sadness. You therefore won't have happiness all the time, and trying to force happiness will only cause existing negative thoughts to entrench themselves more deeply in your psyche.

Positivity is not about what emotions you feel; it is still fully possible for a positive person to cry, or to shout or to sulk, even if they're less likely to do these things than negative people. A positive person is defined not by how they feel, but rather by how they choose to deal with the way they feel, and how they choose to share that feeling with others.

Therefore, the five people you choose to keep closest to you do not have to be the ones who smile or laugh the most. Likewise, you do not need to stress about being happy all the time to achieve positivity. A person who is truly feeling confident in any given moment does not think about questioning whether or not he or she is confident. A person who is upset does not wonder whether or not they are feeling upset. A person who is happy isn't stressing, worrying, or wondering about whether or not they're happy. A happy person simply *is*.

Extending from this, a person seeking happiness will have a great deal of trouble finding it. Happiness can be discerned, but cannot be manufactured. This is because happiness isn't a thing, nor does it live in things. It's simply an emotional response we have depending on other factors going on in our lives. And then, like any other emotion, we'll feel it briefly before we go back to normal.

Building on this, things we enjoy don't necessarily bring happiness. You can enjoy sex, but if you value romance, you won't feel happy unless your romantic life as a whole is in order. You can enjoy food, but you won't feel happy if you aren't sure when you'll next be able to eat, nor will you feel great if your joy is being accompanied by a sense of guilt.

Buying a new car may lead to an enjoyable driving experience, binging alcohol might give you an enjoyable buzz, but in both cases you'll still have to face the next day knowing you blew money on something you didn't need and that doesn't support your values. And then you will not feel happy.

And then, completing the triangle, the things we enjoy aren't what determine our positivity. However, being positive makes you more likely to experience happiness in what you enjoy. Being positive also makes you feel less dependent on happiness, as some of the most common compulsions for seeking happiness—less stress, more satisfaction with life—are already fulfilled by a positive mindset. And what makes a positive mindset isn't what you own; it lies in your ability to connect with others, your ability to process experiences so that you learn even from failures. Positivity is a habit of striving to be empathic and self-aware, and of striving to turn anything that bothers you in life into an opportunity to reflect on what truly matters to you.

So, we cannot gain positivity by relying on things, and we do not depend on happiness for positivity either. Positivity is something we can form in ourselves at any time, although having people around us who support this way of thinking always makes things easier. However, what happens if I am experiencing a negative emotion? How do I deal with that feeling in a positive way?

Even the people we love, the people we draw our positive energy from, will upset us from time to time. In some cases, such as loss, their absence will cause us no end of grief. Forgiveness, as mentioned earlier, is one of the best tools for dealing with negative emotions in a positive manner. But what if we do not feel ready to forgive?

Firstly, recognize that being positive doesn't mean you need to feel positive 100% of the time. Once again, it's not about what you feel, it's about how you choose to deal with it. Not how you dealt with it in the past, or how you will deal with it in the future; how you are dealing with it now, in this very moment. No one is perfect, and believing you aren't allowed to falter in order to be defined as positive will only put you in a negative mindset.

When you're dealing with negative emotions, it's wise to instead perform a value-check on yourself. Ask yourself, "What is important to me in life? How do I spend my time? What do I make time for in my life?" and then, finally, "Do these actions align with what I believe to be right?"

Consider what you believe to be right, and then do your best to express your negative emotion in the context of that value. There is nothing wrong with experiencing negativity. However, negative feelings or experiences can pull us down if we act on them without keeping our values in mind, whether we value peace, family, love, honor, or integrity. When dealing with a bad feeling while keeping what matters to us in mind, however, it can transform into a building block for us to construct a stronger life on.

9

ESCAPE THE VICTIM MENTALITY

While it is true that our friends can help us feel more positive, it does not then follow that they're responsible for our positivity. As the saying goes, you can lead a horse to water, but you cannot make it drink.

A good selection of friends can encourage and support your efforts to grow as a person and find greater joy in all aspects of life, but ultimately you are the one responsible for constructing and maintaining that mindset. You are the architect of your soul.

In wealthy societies, and for many individuals raised in a consumerist culture, one's life is so full of things that it's difficult to decide what to care about anymore. This can, in turn, make it harder to determine our values which, in turn, can make dealing with difficult experiences in a positive manner much trickier than they otherwise would be.

Complicating matters further is how positivity is marketed towards us. As nice as it is, it is unhealthy to try to pursue positivity all the time.

It is healthy to know what you want, and it is good to establish relations with those who are supportive of you. However, you must be careful not to let your goals devolve into a vague or abstract desire for "positivity." When we do that, we tend to then fall into the trap of obsessively pursuing joy or happiness.

Now, there's nothing wrong with experiencing joy or happiness; they're both wonderful things to feel. However, remember what was said earlier; the happy person isn't trying to be happy. They simply are. Happiness, joy and even positivity are all like wild animals that you're trying to soothe and tame.

You won't catch it if you try to chase it; in fact, in chasing it you're more likely to kill it than tame it. The best you can do, then, is encourage it to come to you. This is why Chapter 8 encourages you to invite positivity into your life by being aware of what you want and making time to interact with people who have similar interests. Friendship with those who genuinely value and care about you is a wonderful thing and an amazing way to entice positivity into our lives! But what if we try to chase positivity directly?

When we cultivate a powerful desire to chase positivity, we only make ourselves more aware of the negativity in our lives. In extreme cases, it can even blind you to the good that you already have. Think of any of the more obsessive corporate climbers you may know, who pursue wealth only to never feel quite rich enough despite earning a 6-figure salary and potentially possessing thousands, or even millions of dollars in assets.

Likewise, think of the individual who pursues someone without taking to account what we discussed in Chapter 8. They'll work hard to make themselves attractive, and yet in the end they'll only make themselves feel ugly and unwanted because they keep trying to interface with someone who doesn't hold the same values. They'll feel unwanted, even when they're adored by people around them, because when one focuses on the pursuit one tends to tune out what's sitting in one's peripheral vision.

In the same way that obsessively chasing wealth or attractiveness will leave you feeling the opposite, so too will obsessively chasing positivity leave you feeling negative in the long run. In all these cases, you're desiring to fill a perceived emptiness in your life, whether it exists or not. The longer you chase, the worse and more real this emptiness becomes.

So think of positivity not as a matter of desire or pursuit, but rather as a matter of appreciation. When you let yourself experience appreciation for what's around you, and when you allow that appreciation to enter your core as a human being, you'll naturally invite positivity into your life in a healthy and long-lasting manner. Cherish the good things that already exist in your life, and positivity will naturally manifest itself around you without you having to chase it. This is because instead of trying to fill a perceived emptiness with external things, you're instead taking stock of the fullness that already exists in your life.

But what about the negativity that exists in one's life? Although counter-intuitive, accepting negativity can lead to greater positivity in the long run, just like how focusing too much on chasing "positive" things could make us feel worse.

But what does it mean to accept negativity? Accepting negativity does not mean being pessimistic. Rather, it means realizing that bad things will happen occasionally and that, while one must do what they can about it according to their true values (remember that rest, comfort and self-care are values too), it's not worth getting ensnared by it.

To accept negativity, then, does not mean letting oneself be surrounded by it. Rather, accepting negativity means being conscious of its existence, and then being okay with letting it go, similarly to how you'd let go of a bad thought spiral during meditation. Letting go doesn't mean denial; it means acknowledgment, followed by the assertion that your current thoughts and feelings do not have to define your entire reality. Thoughts and feelings can change easily from one moment to the next, and yet reality carries on around us as it always does.

ESTABLISHING AGENCY

So, why was all of the above relevant in terms of escaping the victim mentality? What's hopefully clear by now is that reality is what it is, no matter how we choose to think or feel about it. That said, we *do* have the power to change the way we interact with that reality. We also have the power to change which part of that reality we're most often surrounded by. Furthermore, it is our own behavior that determines whether we remain a victim or become an active living body once again. And, finally, just because we have been behaving like a victim for the past few days, months or years doesn't mean it's too late to start looking at the world differently.

Now, this is not to say that everything bad that happens to you is your fault; it's not. I know for my grief, it was not my choice to lose my mother. I was powerless to stop that. However, I began to feel powerless all the time. Every time something bad happened, such as a teacher snapping at a student and giving them detention for a minor accident, being turned down for multiple job interviews despite having good grades and hearty letters of recommendation, people making unwelcome comments on my appearance... I just accepted these things, thinking the world was an awful place and that nothing could be done to change it.

Although the world can be awful, my budding victim mentality fooled me into thinking all of it was awful, all the time.

A victim mentality is one of the most disempowering things you can have. It is a form of deep pessimism that encourages you to believe that just because you cannot control some of the things in your life, you are therefore unable to control anything in your life. This is a logical fallacy. I might not be able to control whether it is raining or not, but I can control whether or not I bring an umbrella or thermal jacket when I step outside. I might not be able to control when I feel happy or joyful, but I can control whether I surround myself with people that I value, or participate in events that line up with my principles.

Likewise, thinking back, I could've spoken to the teacher and shown them compassion by asking how their day has been. If I had a major problem with the punishment of the student, I could've talked to the student council or even the principal. And if they wouldn't listen, I could've talked to the student and their parents and offered sympathy, and if the issue was worth kicking a fuss up about, I could've helped them do that too. There's always some way for us to change our circumstances, and even the smallest steps are better than taking none at all. When I was grieving, I wanted help, sympathy and support, but I was blind to the fact that everyone around me needed these things too. As much as I was willing to get, I needed to also be willing to give before I could experience true healing.

Eventually, I found a job by remaining persistent and keeping an open mind in case an unexpected opportunity came up, and being heckled on the street didn't matter once I realized that the opinions of strangers have no inherent power over me and I don't have to care what they think.

We are not perpetual victims. Although we may be tricked, hit, bamboozled, and hurt, the victimhood incurred by such actions is temporary. While it is important to let yourself feel the emotions associated with being betrayed or attacked, endeavor to never use these feelings as an excuse to stop striving for the kind of life you want, or the values you believe in.

What you want or value can change over time, of course; the more we learn, the more our conscious values change as we grow closer to our true selves, so there's no shame in conceding a belief. The point is that when we make the choice to change, it should always be for the sake of growth and life, not for the sake of shrinking into our own shadows.

When examining the functionally positive and successful people around you, you might notice that when something bad happens in their lives, they will take some measure of responsibility for it. A newly promoted manager who goes, "Argh, I'm being swamped by so much work all of a sudden! The corporation doesn't care about me, treating me like some dumb cog in their dumb machine. This job sucks!" isn't going to be a manager for long, or at least not a very good one. The kind of attitude shown above tends to lead to laziness, cantankerous behavior and a scared or demotivated workforce.

In contrast, imagine a newly promoted manager saying, "Wow, this is a hell of a lot of work compared to what I'm used to, but I guess that's what it takes to do this job. Well, they wouldn't have promoted me if they didn't think I was ready, so I'll give it a try and do the best I can."

Unlike the first manager, this manager isn't boxing themselves into the victim mentality. Out of the two managers, which one do you think sounds most likely to approach a colleague if they need help? The one who wants to do the best they can, or the one who believes that they're seen as just a lonely cog in an unfeeling machine? Out of the two managers, which one do you think is more likely to speak honestly (read: without shifting blame or hiding the issue behind flattery or excuses) and seek support from their supervisors if things aren't going well? The one who assumes their supervisors don't care and are out to get them, or the one who believes their supervisors want to see them succeed?

Out of the two managers, which one is more likely to get the help they need and achieve success? The one who chooses to communicate with their superiors and interface with their colleagues, of course! Trust me when I tell you that a person who compares themselves to a powerless cog in their own narratives and assumes everyone is against them *isn't* going to be the one who'll effectively gain this help, even if they need it.

YOU HAVE POWER OVER YOUR FATE

Even if the 2 managers above were equal in all other aspects, that difference in attitude is what would've made the difference between success and failure. In both cases, they can't control that they've just been given a large workload, but they can control how they perceive the issue at hand, which in turn can subtly influence how they go about resolving it.

Even if the task truly is insurmountable, the manager who has avoided victim mentality won't take failure or even demotion personally; they'll simply return to what they know they're good at and keep practicing it until another opportunity for growth presents itself. The manager who has avoided victim mentality is also less likely to lash out or become embittered with those around them, meaning even though things didn't go so well, they at least haven't completely shut the door on trying again.

When you accept that you can take charge of your life, even if it's just some aspects of it, you not only become more powerful in your personal affairs, you become more charismatic, as giving yourself direction makes it easier for you to direct others when they are unsure or confused.

When you are stuck with the victim mentality, however, you depend on people completely and utterly to do things for you. This is fine for short periods, but people will struggle to help you for long when you're this dependent, as most won't know what you truly want. And when they don't know what you want, they're far more likely to return to sorting out their own lives than guess at how to resolve yours. Usually, only parents have the patience to guess what the problem is in cases like this, and even then only when dealing with infants or small children who can't be expected to communicate effectively yet.

In contrast, when you're able to acknowledge responsibility for your life, people find it much easier to assist you when you feel stuck because you're at least acting as the driving force in your own narrative, rather than forcing them to do it.

When you maintain the drive to guide or lead sympathetic efforts in your own life as you resolve personal issues, people feel more secure that what they're doing for you matters, and that you'd be able to help them in turn if they needed it. They render their aid to you feeling warm and satisfied, and a feeling of appreciation forms between you both, contributing to healthy positivity.

On the other hand, when we consistently sit around and list off all our own aches, pains and grievances without exploring ways to solve them on our own time, we end up becoming psychological vampires who drain anyone who comes near us of their time and energy, leaving them feeling tired and empty rather than satisfied. We also end up becoming more entitled if such a victim mentality persists long enough on our part, since we grow more and more accustomed to people simply swooping in and magically fixing all our problems without us having to do anything more than complain.

That said, if you are currently suffering from victim mentality, do not stress. By taking control of small things in your life, but realizing that not everything needs to be interfered with, and you'll come closer to breaking free of your victim mentality.

By being aware of your emotional wants and needs, but recognizing it is better to invite than to chase, you break free of your victim mentality. By being forgiving, you break free; blaming people less means you assign responsibility to others less, meaning you are less likely to construct self-destructive narratives where they hold all the power and you have no say. You become less likely to trap yourself mentally. Writing, reading, exercising and meditating all encourage you to empower yourself, take some action in your life–even if it's small–and thus break free of perpetual victimhood.

Those who suffer from grief are victims, but not forever. By avoiding the cultivation of a perpetual victim mentality, you reduce your chances of worsening into complicated grief, and from there remain in a better position to address what truly matters to you in the way that *you* want to address it. Victim mentality forces us to grieve on everyone else's timetable, but proper healing through grief requires us to take time for ourselves.

10

ACCEPT RESPONSIBILITY FOR YOURSELF

To ensure you stay free of perpetual victim-mentality, however, you need to take more and more responsibility for your own wellbeing—whether that is physical, emotional or intellectual.

Remember when we spoke about how amazingly awesome positive friends can be? We also touched on how it is nevertheless poor form to hold them responsible for our positivity. In the end, working towards your positivity requires a series of choices that must be made personally by you.

However, I don't think we've fully explored what the consequences can be when we do place the responsibility for our wellbeing in the hands of others.

ACCEPT RESPONSIBILITY FOR YOUR EMOTIONS

When we believe a person, most commonly a lover or spouse, is responsible for the way we feel, we tend to blame them for *our* negative emotions. Yet, when we blame someone else for what we feel, strange things start to happen.

Firstly, when we make a person responsible for the way we feel, we also imply that we are responsible for the way they feel too. This is because one-sided responsibility strongly resembles a parent-child relationship. This isn't a functional way for adults to relate to one another, so most people who want the relationship to continue when they're blamed for their partner's emotions will start blaming their partner in turn. This leads to, and reinforces, emotional codependency between the two partners.

However, this mutual codependence doesn't make things better. When we hold each other responsible for how we feel, rather than ourselves, we both become more likely to enter the victim mentality together. Personal boundaries fly out the window, but in a way that is scary and constrictive rather than sexy or intimate.

This leads to a situation where neither partner feels safe doing *anything* without the approval of the other. Whether it's deciding on dinner, deciding what to watch on TV or even deciding how to spend alone time when apart, everything eventually ends up being cross-checked. Our lives eventually revolve around the emotional wellbeing of the other.

Now, it is natural to care for one another in any form of relationship, whether romantic or platonic. This is normal and healthy. However, when this care is not only taken for granted, but *expected* to be prioritized 24/7, then there will invariably be great resentments. When we start getting mad at someone close to us because they fail to be fully devoted to us 24/7, then not only are we making the mistake of assuming them to be perfect or divine (and also making the mistake of assuming that what's perfect for us is perfect for everyone), we're also being extraordinarily selfish by refusing to consider what is going on in *their* lives that might be distracting or upsetting them.

Likewise, we can become bitter towards someone if they treat us this way too, and this bitterness not only leads to otherwise avoidable conflicts and grief, it can also encourage us to form bad habits (such as manipulation) as we resort to do anything to satisfy our partner's feelings or desires, even if that "satisfaction" is brought about by a combination of guilt, shame and trickery.

When we create an environment where love or support is given out of *obligation* or *expectation* rather than *choice*, we also create an environment that encourages us to hide how we truly feel and manipulate what we think our partner feels.

When we accept responsibility for our own feelings, however, and trust our partner to do the same, we make room in our lives for freely-given love. Freely-given love between two people creates an environment where we don't automatically assume the worst of our partner just because they aren't being especially supportive on a given day. Instead of weaving a narrative where they're heartless or insensitive, in a situation of freely-given love we are more likely to be honest with our emotions and ask for help if we need it.

ACCEPT RESPONSIBILITY FOR YOUR OWN STANDARDS

Remember, accepting responsibility for yourself is the antithesis of being trapped in a perpetual malaise of victimhood. Part of this involves accepting responsibility for your standards: the metrics by which you judge others or judge yourself.

It's always important to criticize our metrics, as the ways we choose to measure ourselves aren't always realistic. You can be a smart, funny and good-looking individual, yet still feel stupid, boring or ugly because of a self-limiting value metric.

For instance, maybe you grew up to be much shorter than you expected. Maybe, because you're shorter than most people you know, you feel ugly and that no one will ever love you. This is an example of an extremely limiting belief; when we define our worth based on a system of measurement we have no control over, we disempower ourselves. It's not your fault that you're short. It's not something you chose. So, why define your self-worth based on your height? Out of all your other qualities, why *height?* Would you judge others based solely on the distance between their head and the ceiling? Probably not, because most of us realize how superficial such a measurement system is when applied to others. So why are we applying it to ourselves?

Maybe you aren't as muscular as you would like to be. This is something you have some choice over, but despite valuing muscles maybe you don't value the processes behind muscle-building enough to follow through, causing an inner conflict. To help resolve this conflict, think of the best people in your life. Is it their muscles that made them such wonderful people? Even for athletes, the appearance of their muscles isn't as important as what those muscles let them do on the field, and only then because it's important to their passion and career. If you judged all your friends primarily by their muscles, you'd certainly miss out on a treasure trove of their deeper qualities. Likewise, judging yourself by such a metric could make you miss out on yours.

When you find that your standards are bringing you down or making you feel inferior, it is best to perform a value-check on yourself. In the case of our hypothetical height scenario, why do you value the idea of being tall? Usually, one values the idea of being tall because we feel it makes us attractive. However, being tall isn't the only way to be attractive. In that case, someone who felt ugly because they're short could overcome their limiting belief by exploring other ways of being attractive; being clever, witty, or interesting. Overcoming a limiting belief also makes you inherently more attractive, since it helps you feel more secure in yourself and avoid being the psychological vampire we mentioned earlier. On the physical side, there's also nothing stopping you from keeping yourself well-groomed or pulling off a rugged charm; these qualities are independent of height.

In the muscle scenario, why do you value the idea of being strong? The 3 biggest reasons tend to be, "I want to look more attractive", "I want to be healthier", and "I want to get better at protecting those I care about". Not everyone builds muscles as easily; bodybuilders in particular MUST live by a very strict diet that is neither practical nor enjoyable for most people. In the case of attractiveness, see the previous paragraph. In the case of being healthier, why are muscles important for that? If you aren't getting sick that often, and are fit enough to accomplish the work of your average day while remaining in a good mood, then you're healthy, regardless of your muscle mass.

In the case of protection, your mind is much more important than your muscles; tactics, technique, quick-thinking, perception, preparation will all help you protect yourself without you needing great strength at all. Don't get caught up in surface goals like, "I want to be richer, stronger, more beautiful, more powerful." Always ask yourself WHY you want these things, and then think of alternate ways to satisfy that root motivation. If you can't think of alternate ways, borrow a book on subjects similar to your root motive. There are always options for achieving a root goal.

This also goes for when the root goal is something like becoming smarter, discovering something new, finding inner peace or cultivating love; the large number of viable religious, philosophical and political belief systems show this quite handily, as if the wide and diverse fields of knowledge available in the world didn't demonstrate that on its own.

When we question the root cause of our standards and values, we're able to change and improve them for the better. It also makes it easier for us to play to our strengths, since considering the reasoning behind our standards makes it easier for us to find alternative ways to achieve the aim that our standards were intended to encourage.

The values and metrics by which you measure yourself are entirely your choices. While you can blame others for encouraging you to think or measure yourself a certain way, in the end you are the one responsible for changing how you think if you don't believe it's working. No matter what people have done or how they behaved in the past, you are responsible for what you choose to do next in life.

ACCEPT RESPONSIBILITY FOR YOUR PROBLEMS

It wasn't my fault that I had to deal with grief over my mother, but it was still my responsibility to deal with it. I am responsible for the choices I made. I am responsible for how I felt.

It wasn't my dad's fault that he had to deal with grief over my mother either, but it was still his responsibility to continue being a parent and raise me. Now, technically, all he had to do was keep me alive and attending school. In his grief, he could've chosen to do not an ounce more than that. However, responsibility doesn't just apply to what we're expected to do, it applies to anything we have some measure of power or control over, and while people might not blame us beyond our obligations, all of our responsibilities carry wider consequences. If my dad couldn't accept his wider, unobligated responsibilities and got stuck in a victim mentality, school would've been a lot harder for me. We might've even lost the house, and an already difficult situation would have spiraled into something much worse as a result. But, because he continued being responsible for everything he could still realistically control, my dad made sure that although some parts of life sucked, there'd still be some spaces that were safe and comfortable. He made sure I always had a cozy place to do my homework, and that I always had access to any books or stationery I needed. He also did his best to comfort me, although I didn't always listen. He couldn't control whether or not I sincerely took what he said to heart, but he could control whether or not he'd present the foundations for an epiphany to me. He didn't let my obstinate nature (I was a teen at the time, to be fair) push him into a victim mentality. He just kept focusing on what he could do, and through that brought about positive change.

Going further, it wasn't the doctor's fault that my mother died. Maybe, in his mind, he could've done a better job trying to save her, but from my point of view he'd done everything he could. When terminal illness was confirmed, he could've chosen to act like a victim and believe that, because he couldn't save her, he couldn't do anything else further. Luckily, that's not the choice he made. He recognized that, while he was no longer practically responsible for her life, he was still responsible for her comfort. He couldn't realistically control whether she lived or died, but he could at least make sure she died as painlessly as possible, and that he'd keep giving her the best fighting chance he could until that happened. He could also control whether or not he'd try to comfort us after she passed away. Thanks to his actions, what would otherwise have been a wholly traumatic event at least carried the solace that the people looking after our mother in hospital *cared* for her. It was remembering this act of care that eventually helped me pull myself out of my own state of victim mentality, as it directly challenged my misguided worldview that I lived in a cold and heartless society.

And, of course, it wasn't my mother's fault that she was so ill. This won't be true for everyone that is dying, but whether it's the person's fault or not doesn't matter at that stage; when something is someone's fault, it meant they made a mistake in the past. Responsibility is how we choose to deal with things in the present, regardless of whether they're our fault or not.

For my mother, her responsibility was making the best of her remaining time on this Earth. She seemed to slow down a bit, as if she was now taking the time to truly pay attention to everything, and she managed to smile and laugh a lot more because of this, even though we could all see she was in great pain. She continued enjoying life with us as much as she could, until she was bedridden in the hospital and it became our responsibility to be there for her. Again, responsibility is not the same as obligation; we could've chosen to just leave her there and begin grieving immediately. We weren't legally or even socially obligated by anyone to go see her during her stay in the hospital once she was admitted. But we valued her, and although we couldn't control whether or not she lived another day, we could control whether or not we pitched up and made ourselves part of those last days.

Because we chose to act on what we could control, we could at least say goodbye, and had plenty of opportunities to share corny jokes and anecdotes from her life I'd otherwise never known.

Because she chose to act on what she could control, she helped lay a positive foundation. All these years after the worst of my grief has long departed, I still remember how brave and spirited she was. I still remember the love in her eyes, and I remember how weakly her hand would grab onto mine in her last few days. Her choice to act on what she could control meant that even after she had passed on, there was never a moment of doubt - in my dad's, brother's or my heart- that she loved us dearly, and that she knew we loved her.

Imagine if she'd instead embraced her potential victim mentality; if she used her impending death as an excuse to do nothing, say nothing and just sequester herself away to perish. We'd never have found any closure, and life may have turned out very differently for my dad, brother, and I.

So, as much as possible, take responsibility for the problems that come up in your life. Taking responsibility doesn't mean solving them single-handedly, but it does mean standing up in defiance against the idea that you're powerless. It means acting in whatever small way you can to make life better along the threads that you control. It means accepting that even the smallest positive differences are worth making. Every brush stroke in a painting makes up the artwork. Every layer of paint contributes to the final piece.

So take responsibility for your life as much as you can. Every positive brushstroke you make will help build up the artwork that is your life, so that you can look at it with satisfaction, and that those you love can look at it and find peace.

CONCLUSION

Although this is the end of this book, this is not the end of your journey. Everyone grieves differently, there's no need to rush your healing. However, continue to practice what you've learned as best you can. If you need more answers, do not hesitate to read further from a wide variety of authors; every writer's differing perspective of a topic will help you build a more universal view.

To solidify that view and order the chaotic thoughts one often experiences during grief, remember to ink down the breathings of your heart. No matter how you feel about something, spending a few minutes writing about it can help you spot patterns you may have otherwise missed. And, when the subject matter becomes too heavy or overwhelming even to write through, take a breather by sitting down and letting yourself meditate for a few minutes.

Do the best you can to look after yourself physically; make proper time for sleep so that your body and mind both get the rest they need to function properly. Drink liquids, eat food, and move your body so that you begin to feel better each day. Let the oxygen in your blood flow freely through your veins. Scrape the rust off your joints with stretches so that you don't have to fight your body as well as your grief.

As much as you can, be honest about how you feel, both in your writing and in your speech. In times of trouble, keep your five favorite people as close to you as you can, and don't be afraid to hire professional assistance to fill in the gaps.

But most of all, remember that how you deal with grief is on you. The people around you can support and help you, but in the end the decision to heal is down to you. This means you can take as long as you need to heal, regardless of what others say. But it also means you're responsible for the consequences of what you do; if something goes wrong, you're the most reliable person to fix it. If you don't know how to fix it, you're the most reliable person to find someone who can.

The important thing is that you never forget you're allowed to take charge of your life, and you're especially allowed to take charge of how you deal with your grief. The advice in this book simply consists of some of the healthier ways that I found worked for me, based on more than a decade of almost getting it right and then messing up spectacularly.

I compiled all I have learned in the hope that you won't mess up as much, but even if you do, the next important thing is that you never give up. The moment you give up is the moment you stop taking charge of your own healing. The moment you get back up again is the moment you come closer to achieving the life you want.

Don't waste energy chasing after things that can be gained through self-reflection. Don't disempower yourself by blaming others for how you feel and, if you ever do blame someone else, dare to make amends as best you can, both for your sake and for theirs. However, don't blame yourself either. Not everything bad in life has to be assigned as someone's fault. This grief isn't your fault, it isn't anyone's fault. But it is your responsibility. It's like a baby on your doorstep; it may not have come about by your actions, but its fate is now in your hands. So, most of all, be gentle with it.

If you have found this book helpful, please consider helping others by leaving a review on Amazon. I'll be happy to read it and learn from your perspective, much as I hope you've learned from mine. Others who are looking for answers will also use your review to help guide them to where they need to be, so it truly would be appreciated.

It's been my pleasure to share this knowledge with you. Now, go forth and use it to help your world shine light through the rains of grief.

REFERENCES

Ackerman, C. (2020, February 11). *Trauma-Focused Cognitive Behavioral Therapy: Life After Freud.* PositivePsychology.Com.

https://positivepsychology.com/trauma-focused-cognitive-behavioral-therapy/

Aqtai, A. (2019). Brown Desk Lamp on Table. In *Pexels*.

https://www.pexels.com/photo/brown-desk-lamp-on-table-2233416/

Ardagh, P. (2008). *Philip Ardagh's Book of Absolutely Useless Lists for Absolutely Every Day of the Year.* Macmillan.

ArtHouse Studio. (2020). Relaxed Woman in White Bathrobe Reading Ebook. In *Pexels.* https://www.pexels.com/photo/relaxed-woman-in-white-bathrobe-reading-ebook-4353680/

Baikie, K., & Wilhelm, K. (2005). Emotional and Physical Health Benefits of Expressive Writing. *Advances in Psychiatric Treatment*, 11(5), 338–346.

https://doi.org/10.1192/apt.11.5.338

Bernardo, C. (2016, January 5). *Grief and Nutrition: Tips From a Wellness Guru*. What's Your Grief.

https://whatsyourgrief.com/grief-and-nutrition/

Bertelli, M. (2017). Woman Using Umbrella With Lights. In *Pexels*.

https://www.pexels.com/photo/astronomy-dark-dawn-dusk-573238/

Brown, L. F., Reynolds, C. F., Monk, T. H., Prigerson, H. G., Dew, M. A., Houck, P. R., Mazumdar, S., Buysse, D. J., Hoch, C. C., & Kupfer, D. J. (1996). Social Rhythm Stability Following Late-Life Spousal Bereavement: Associations With Depression and Sleep Impairment. *Psychiatry Research*, 62(2), 161–169.

https://doi.org/10.1016/0165-1781(96)02914-9

Buxbaum, J. (2016, April 1). *8 Unexpected Ways Books Can Help You Through Grief*. Bustle.

https://www.bustle.com/articles/151288-8-unexpected-ways-books-can-help-you-through-grief-and-loss

Cherney, K. (2018, November 66). *How Long Does Caffeine Stay in Your System?* Healthline; Healthline Media.

https://www.healthline.com/health/how-long-does-caffeine-last

Colier, N. (2018, January 12). *Are You Ready to Stop Feeling Like a Victim?* Psychology Today. https://www.psychologytoday.com/ca/blog/inviting-monkey-tea/201801/are-you-ready-stop-feeling-victim

Constance, K. (2019). Woman Sitting on Wooden Planks. In *Pexels*.

https://www.pexels.com/photo/woman-sitting-on-wooden-planks-2865901/

Cottonbro. (2020a). Sticky Notes on Glass Wall. In *Pexels*.

https://www.pexels.com/photo/sticky-notes-on-glass-wall-3831847/

Cottonbro. (2020b). Person in Black Pants and Black Shoes Sitting on Brown Wooden Chair. In *Pexels*.

https://www.pexels.com/photo/person-in-black-pants-and-black-shoes-sitting-on-brown-wooden-chair-4101143/

Cushner, K. (2018, March 12). *How to Fall Back Asleep If You Wake Up.* Tuck Sleep.

https://www.tuck.com/fall-back-asleep/

Denis E. Boyd & Associates Inc. (2020). *Brooke Lewis*. Denis Boyd & Associates Psychologists & Counsellors.

https://www.denisboyd.com/about-us/therapists/brooke-lewis/

DeNoon, D. J. (2008, May 30). *Exercise and Depression*. WebMD.

https://www.webmd.com/depression/guide/exercise-depression#1

Domingues, C. (2017). Closeup Photography of Adult Short-Coated Tan and White Dog Sleeping on Gray Textile at Daytime. In *Pexels*.

https://www.pexels.com/photo/closeup-photography-of-adult-short-coated-tan-and-white-dog-sleeping-on-gray-textile-at-daytime-731022/

Frey, M. (2019, May 27). *Exercise and Nutrition Tips to Ease the Grieving Process*. Verywell Fit.

https://www.verywellfit.com/exercise-and-nutrition-tips-to-ease-the-grieving-process-4160071

Frey, M. (2020, May 29). *8 Easy Workouts for Beginners*. Verywell Fit.

https://www.verywellfit.com/easy-weight-loss-workouts-for-beginners-3495986

Fring, G. (2020a). Man Lying With Journal Sharing Problems With Advisor. In *Pexels*.

https://www.pexels.com/photo/man-lying-with-journal-sharing-problems-with-advisor-4148892/

Fring, G. (2020b). Smiling Students Discussing Day in College. In *Pexels*.

https://www.pexels.com/photo/smiling-students-discussing-day-in-college-4172961/

Goncharenok, M. (2020). Photo of Man Lying on Concrete Floor. In *Pexels*.

https://www.pexels.com/photo/photo-of-man-lying-on-concrete-floor-4663822/

Harvey, S. B., Øverland, S., Hatch, S. L., Wessely, S., Mykletun, A., & Hotopf, M. (2017). Exercise and the Prevention of Depression: Results of the HUNT Cohort Study. *American Journal of Psychiatry*, 175(1), 28–36.

https://doi.org/10.1176/appi.ajp.2017.16111223

Hotchandani, E. (2020). *Home | Eric Hotchandani | Marriage and Family Counseling.* Eric Hotchandani, LMFT.

https://www.erichotchandani.com/

Hugstad, K. (2017, June 19). *What to Eat When Grief Is Eating You*. HuffPost. https://www.huffpost.com/entry/what-to-eat-when-grief-is-eating-you_b_59481460e4b0f7875b83e4ad

Inouye, M. (2019). Self Care Isn't Selfish Signage. In *Pexels*.

https://www.pexels.com/photo/self-care-isn-t-selfish-signage-2821823/

Jewell, T. (2014, January 22). *Depression vs. Complicated Grief*. Healthline; Healthline Media.

https://www.healthline.com/health/depression/complicated-grief#symptoms

Kaboompics.com. (2015). Woman's Hand Using a Pen Noting on Notepad. In *Pexels*. https://www.pexels.com/photo/woman-s-hand-using-a-pen-noting-on-notepad-6360/

Kentish-Barnes, N., Chaize, M., Seegers, V., Legriel, S., Cariou, A., Jaber, S., Lefrant, J.-Y., Floccard, B., Renault, A., Vinatier, I., Mathonnet, A., Reuter, D., Guisset, O., Cohen-Solal, Z., Cracco, C., Seguin, A., Durand-Gasselin, J., Éon, B., Thirion, M., ... Azoulay, É. (2015). Complicated Grief After Death of a Relative in the Intensive Care Unit. *European Respiratory Journal*, 45(5), 1341–1352.

https://doi.org/10.1183/09031936.00160014

Kilroy, D. (2019, February 27). *Eating the Right Foods for Exercise*. Healthline; Healthline Media.

https://www.healthline.com/health/fitness-exercise-eating-healthy#carbohydrates

Knott, L. (2017, September 11). Depression. Patient.

https://patient.info/mental-health/depression-leaflet

Kornfield, J. (2017, September 13). *A Meditation on Grief.* Jack Kornfield.

https://jackkornfield.com/meditation-grief/

Kos, B. (2016, March 10). *Why You Should Read Every Day.* AgileLeanLife.

https://agileleanlife.com/why-you-should-read-every-day/

Lehman, S. (2020, April 1). *An Overview of Nutrition for a Better Diet.* Verywell Fit.

https://www.verywellfit.com/nutrition-basics-4157080

Manson, M. (2020). *Personal Values: A Guide to Figuring Out Who You Are.* Mark Manson.

https://markmanson.net/values/personal-values-guide

Neimeyer, R., Hardison, H., & Lichstein, K. (2005). Insomnia and Complicated Grief Symptoms in Bereaved College Students. *Behavioral Sleep Medicine,* 3(2), 99–111.

https://doi.org/10.1207/s15402010bsm0302_4

Pasternak, R. E., Reynolds, C. F., Hoch, C. C., Buysse, D. S., Schlernitzauer, M., Machen, M., & Kupfer, D. J. (1992). Sleep in Spousally Bereaved Elders With Subsyndromal Depressive Symptoms. *Psychiatry Research*, 43(1), 43–53.

https://doi.org/10.1016/0165-1781(92)90140-x

Piacquadio, A. (2020a). Woman Draw a Light Bulb in White Board. In *Pexels*.

https://www.pexels.com/photo/woman-draw-a-light-bulb-in-white-board-3758105/

Piacquadio, A. (2020b). Photo of Man in Gray T-Shirt and Black Jeans on Sitting on Wooden Floor Meditating. In *Pexels*.

https://www.pexels.com/photo/photo-of-man-in-gray-t-shirt-and-black-jeans-on-sitting-on-wooden-floor-meditating-3760611/

Salla, S. (2019, April 1). *#8 Ways to Surround Yourself With Positive Energy*. Entrepreneur.

https://www.entrepreneur.com/article/331564

Sample, I. (2009, February 15). *Keeping a Diary Makes You Happier*. The Guardian.

https://www.theguardian.com/science/2009/feb/15/psychology-usa

Sayles, B. (2019). Two Men and Woman Sitting Next to Each Other. In *Pexels*.

https://www.pexels.com/photo/two-men-and-woman-sitting-next-to-each-other-2479312/

Scott, E. (2020, February 13). *4 Ways to Surround Yourself With Positive Energy*. Verywell Mind.

https://www.verywellmind.com/reduce-stress-positive-energy-3144815

Singh, Y. (2018). Man Walking Near Body of Water. In *Pexels*.

https://www.pexels.com/photo/man-walking-near-body-of-water-1466852/

Smith, L. (2018, May 16). *Can Exercise Help Those Dealing With Grief?* Patient.

https://patient.info/news-and-features/can-exercise-help-with-grief

Snapwire. (2017). Close-Up Photography of Lighted Candles. In *Pexels*.

https://www.pexels.com/photo/close-up-photography-of-lighted-candles-722653/

Stang, H. (2020, April 19). *Grief Journaling Tips & Writing Prompts for Meaning Making After Loss*. Mindfulness & Grief.

https://mindfulnessandgrief.com/grief-journaling/

Stutzer, A. (2018, March 22). *How Does Your Smartphone Affect Your Sleep?* Tuck Sleep.

https://www.tuck.com/smartphones-and-sleep/

Tartakovsky, M. (2019, June 7). Benefits of Therapy You Probably Didn't Know About. PsychCentral.

https://psychcentral.com/blog/benefits-of-therapy-you-probably-didnt-know-about/

Tentis, D. (2017). Cooked Meat With Vegetables. In *Pexels*.

https://www.pexels.com/photo/cooked-meat-with-vegetables-725991/

The Survival Journal Editorial Staff. (2020). The Survival Rule of Threes. The Survival Journal.

https://thesurvivaljournal.com/survival-rule-of-threes/

Tran, B. (2018). Dont Wish for It Work for It Calligraphy. In *Pexels*.

https://www.pexels.com/photo/dont-wish-for-it-work-for-it-calligraphy-1074920/

Tuck Sleep. (2019a, July 18). *The Best and Worst Foods for a Good Night's Sleep.* Tuck Sleep.

https://www.tuck.com/foods-that-help-you-sleep/

Tuck Sleep. (2019b, July 21). *Sleep Deprivation - Causes, Dangers, Prevention, Treatment.* Tuck Sleep.

https://www.tuck.com/sleep-deprivation/

Tuck Sleep. (2020a, January 9). *Create an Ideal Environment for Sleep.* Tuck Sleep.

https://www.tuck.com/optimize-your-sleep-environment/

Tuck Sleep. (2020b, March 31). *Health Benefits of Napping.* Tuck Sleep.

https://www.tuck.com/napping/

Tuck Sleep. (2020c, April 22). *Women and Insomnia: Menopause, Pregnancy, and PMS.* Tuck Sleep.

https://www.tuck.com/sleep-disorders/insomnia-women/

Tuck Sleep. (2020d, May 5). *Grief and Sleep Issues: How to Sleep Better During Bereavement.* Tuck Sleep.

https://www.tuck.com/sleep-and-grief/

Tuck Sleep. (2020e, May 18). *Ultimate Guide to Melatonin and Sleep.* Tuck Sleep.

https://www.tuck.com/melatonin/

Wong, C. (2020, February 3). *The 20 Best Food Sources of Antioxidants.* Verywell Fit.

https://www.verywellfit.com/best-food-sources-of-antioxidants-88392

Zakri, J. (2020, March 31). *What Is Sleep Hygiene? Plus 15 Tips for Better Sleep Hygiene*. Tuck Sleep.

https://www.tuck.com/sleep-hygiene/

Zimmerman, P. (2020). Photo of Woman Reading Book. In *Pexels*.

https://www.pexels.com/photo/photo-of-woman-reading-book-3747468/

Printed in Great Britain
by Amazon

54658604R00087